SERIES EDITOR: LEE J

OSPREY MILITARY MEN

LOUIS XV's ARMY (4) LIGHT TROOPS & SPECIALISTS

TEXT BY
RENÈ CHARTRAND

COLOUR PLATES BY
EUGÈNE LELIÈPVRE

OSPREY
MILITARY

First published in Great Britain in 1997 by OSPREY, a division of Reed Books, Michelin House, 81 Fulham Road, London SW3 6RB Auckland and Melbourne

ISBN 1 85532 624 8

Film set in Singapore by Pica Ltd
Printed through World Print Ltd, Hong Kong

Editor: Sharon van der Merwe
Design: TT Design - Stuart Truscott

For a catalogue of all books published by Osprey Military please write to:
Osprey Marketing, Reed Books, Michelin House,
81 Fulham Road, London SW20 6RB

Author's note

This fourth volume in our series of five devoted to the organisation, uniforms and weapons of Louis XV's army, the largest military force in 18th century western Europe, begins by examining the colourful establishment hussars and the many light corps. The generals, staff officers, specialists and military academies are also covered, as are the constabulary corps. Finally, in closing, it will offer a cursory look at the numerous Bourgeois town militia and their uniforms.

The fifth and final volume will cover the colonial troops and militia in New France, the West Indies, Africa and India, as well as marines and other naval troops based in France. It is hoped that this collection of volumes, which includes many contemporary illustrations, portraits and colour plates, will form the most complete account on the organisation and material culture of Louis XV's army published this century.

Publisher's note

Readers may wish to study this title in conjunction with the following Osprey publications:

MAA 296 *Louis XV's Army (1) Cavalry and Dragoons*
MAA 302 *Louis XV's Army (2) French Infantry*
MAA 304 *Louis XV's Army (3) Foreign Infantry*
MAA 285 *King George's Army 1740-93 (1)*
MAA 289 *King George's Army 1740-93 (2)*
MAA 292 *King George's Army 1740-93 (3)*
MAA 236 *Frederick the Great's Army (1) Cavalry*
MAA 240 *Frederick the Great's Army (2) Infantry*
MAA 248 *Frederick the Great's Army (3) Specialist*
MAA 271 *The Austrian Army 1740-80 (1) Cavalry*
MAA 276 *The Austrian Army 1740-80 (2) Infantry*
MAA 280 *The Austrian Army 1740-80 (3) Specialist*
MAA 203 *Louis XIV's Army*

Artist's Note

LOUIS XV's ARMY (4)
LIGHT TROOPS & SPECIALISTS

INTRODUCTION

This fourth instalment of our review of Louis XV's army will reveal an extraordinary variety of units, most now long forgotten, who had a dazzling assortment of uniforms, equipment and weapons. Light troops, bourgeois militia and even the guard companies of senior generals all cultivated their own distinct dress and appearance.

Hussars at the siege of Freibourg, 1744. (Print after Lenfant)

The emergence of light troops at the time of Louis XV's reign is a sign of the search for better intelligence of the enemy and rapid tactical moves on battlefields, which at that time were dominated by ponderous and predictable movements of battalions marching in line in open fields. Light troops were meant to act primarily as skirmishers and raiders to support the main army. Since their tactical role was to be different than that of the bulk of the nation's troops, they were regarded as somewhat exotic. As a result, light troop recruits were often foreigners who, it was believed, brought with them novel ways in the art of war. However, Frenchmen with strong local identities and peculiar fighting methods also qualified – among the latter were various mountain units and the Basque and Breton volunteers. The dress and weaponry of these troops was very distinctive, some of it most unusual, as will be seen in the following pages and illustrations.

HUSSARS

Originating in Hungary, hussars had made their way into the French army by the 1690s as outstanding light cavalry who excelled as skirmishers and patrols. Hussars usually came from Hungary and Germany, recruited by a captain in his native country, but many were deserters

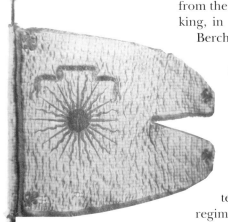

Guidon of Polleresky's Hussars, c.1756-58.

Turpin's Hussars, trooper, c.1757-60.

from the Austrian army's own hussar regiments. When Louis XV became king, in 1715, there were two hussar regiments. They were joined by Bercheny's in 1720, Esterhazy's in 1735 and several more in the 1740s.

The strength of hussar regiments could vary from one to another. In 1740 Bercheny and Linden had two squadrons while Esterhazy had one; each squadron had four companies (three in 1742-48). Companies usually had 25 men in peacetime and 50, sometimes more, in wartime. In 1756 companies were raised to 75 men, but this caused the amalgamation of three regiments into the other three. There could be eight (as in Nassau) or up to 12 companies per regiment (as in Turpin). Each company had a captain, a lieutenant and a cornet (called 'sub-lieutenant' from 1762); each regiment a colonel, a lieutenant-colonel, a major and an aide-major. Companies were reduced to 29 men each in 1762, and from February 1764 each regiment had eight companies.

Since there were relatively few hussar regiments in Louis XV's army, there were probably less than a couple of thousand hussars on the strength in peacetime. In wartime a peak of sorts was reached during the War of Austrian Succession, when, from 1744 to 1748, there were some 4,500 hussars. During the Seven Years War, however, their number peaked at only 2,400, although many were also to be found among the light corps.

The early hussar units dressed in a most unusual style by western European standards of the time. Their costume, usually sky blue and red, was very tight and consisted of a vest called a 'dolman', ornamented with braid, skin-tight breeches with no pockets, a cap with a fur turn-up which by the 1730s had become a fur cap with a bag. The pelisse was initially of wolf's skin, then of cloth edged with fur. Up to the 1720s it was common to find hussars with their head shaved except for one long lock of hair braided on one side. Later on their hair was not shaved but was tied in the queue of the time, though often with braided pleats at each side. Moustaches were *de rigueur* in hussar units.

New regiments raised in the 1730s and early 40s adopted various colours – such as buff and cinnamon – but the authorities insisted upon a return to one standard colour. By royal order of 26 October 1744, all hussar regiments were henceforth to be 'dressed in pelisses, vests [dolmans] and breeches of a sky blue colour, equipped with red housing, leaving only the freedom to the colonels to distinguish [their regiment] by the caps, laces or buttons'. Except for Beaurore's and Lynden's regiments, the hussars adopted sky blue uniforms. Up till the late 1740s hussars mostly wore caps with high fur turn-ups or mirleton conical caps. In December 1747, however, Marshal de Saxe felt that tall conical mirleton caps of white felt were much better. This measure raised protests from hussar general Bercheny. He managed to keep the red caps of his regiment, but others were to have white.

The royal order of 15 May 1752 reinforced the provisions regarding the uniformity of hussar dress. It specified that all regiments were to have sky blue, the dolman with small pointed cuffs of the regimental distinctive colour, sky blue breeches, sky blue pelisse edged with black fur, pewter buttons set in three rows on the dolman and pelisse, white cords,[1] red sash with knots of regimental colour, white felt mirleton caps (except for Bercheny's) with wing lining, fleur de lis and lace of regimental colour, blue cloak, red sabretache with a fleur de lis (and a crown above for Bercheny's) and border edged in the regimental colour, red housings edged with lace of the regimental colour and bearing five white fleurs de lis edged with regimental colour and red leather belts and cartridge box. They were to be armed with a sabre, a pair of M.1733 pistols and a carbine. The white cap, never popular, was finally changed to black in June 1755, with lining of the facing colour (except for Bercheny which kept its red caps).

During the Seven Years War the official uniform remained much the same but there were pressures for change. The new Nassau-Saarbruck Hussar Regiment had dark blue dolmans and breeches with red pelisses while many hussar troops of the light corps (see below) had green.

Towards the end of the war, on 21 December 1762, a totally new uniform was ordered for all hussar regiments. Henceforth the dolman was green, with three rows of buttons and pointed cuffs of the regimental facing colour. There was also a green pelisse edged with black fur, red breeches, pewter buttons, white cords, red sash with facing colour, black cap with wing lining, lace and fleur de lis of the facing colour, green cloak with three laces of the facing colour, red sabretache with fleur de lis and lace edging of the facing colour, and sheepskins with edging of the facing colour. The green uniform remained until 1776.

Hussar officers wore uniforms of the same colours and style but of better materials and with some distinguishing details. The cords, buttons and lace on their uniforms were of silver, increasing in quantity as the rank rose. In 1752 the lace worn by lieutenants was to be 11.2mm wide and that of captains 13.5mm – usually set at the cuffs and on the upper breeches. Their pelisses were edged with grey fox fur. Officers also continued wearing fine quality fur caps (even after the adoption of the felt caps in the 1740s), ornamented with an aigrette – as well as boots of red or yellow leather. Their housings were laced with silver – 40mm wide for captains and 27mm for lieutenants. The senior officers who could afford it had a leopard skin over their saddle. From December 1762 cuffs and breeches lace was 13.5mm wide for sub-lieutenants, 22.5mm for lieutenants and 27mm for captains. Field officers had 22.5mm lace with a row of cord for the major and two for the lieutenant-colonel. The *mestre-de-camp* (colonel) had a 34mm lace and three rows of cords.

Trumpeter and kettledrummer of the Bercheny Hussar Regiment, c.1752-63.

---

1 Many authors, including Marbot and Noirmont, Chopin, Mouilliard and others, have written that the dolman and pelisse cords were of the regimental distinctive colour. The 1752 ordinance, however, clearly states that the cords were to be 'de fil blanc' – 'of white thread'.

The *Maréchal des logis* (senior NCO) had, from 1752 and perhaps earlier, silver lace 9mm wide on the uniform and edging the cap, and 18mm wide lace edging the housings. From December 1762 the lace was replaced by three silk cords for *Maréchal des logis*, two silk cords for 'fourriers' and one of wool for 'brigadiers'.

Musicians in hussar regiments were trumpeters and, rather surprisingly, a kettledrummer per regiment. Kettledrummers were not very compatible with light cavalry and disappeared from the rolls in the 1760s. The dress of musicians was not in the hussar style but in the French fashion, with tricorns, coats with long skirts, false sleeves and wings, and linings of a different colour showing at the cuffs and turnbacks. They wore ordinary French-style waistcoats and breeches, black cavalry boots, pewter buttons and tricorn hats laced with silver. They wore the livery of their colonels. Bercheny's musicians wore brown lined green with white and black livery lace, green waistcoat and buff breeches. Chamborant's were yellow lined sky blue, with sky blue waistcoat and breeches, white livery lace edged black with dark red worm at centre. Royal-Nassau, being 'royal', would have had the king's livery of blue lined red before 1763, and orange later on, with the royal livery lace. Esterhazy's had red with sky blue collar, cuffs and turnbacks, and buff breeches. Unlike other hussars, the trumpeters and kettledrummers were clean shaven and without moustaches. Their hair was usually dressed in the French fashion, although the braided side pleats were also seen.

Count Valentin Stanislas de Esterhazy (1740-1805), colonel of Esterhazy's Hussars, c.1770.

HUSSAR REGIMENTS

Verseilles: Incorporated into Rattsky in May 1716. Sky blue dolman (possibly with small pointed red cuffs), white flat lace, three rows of pewter buttons, red sash, long sky blue breeches, red overalls, wolf-skin pelisse, red cap with fur turn-up and cock's feather, blue cotton shirt, soft leather knee boots and buff sabretache.

Rattsky, 1743 Lynden: Incorporated into Bercheny, Turpin and Polleresky from 30 October 1756. Sky blue dolman (possibly with small pointed red cuffs), white flat lace, three rows of pewter buttons, yellow sash, long sky blue breeches, red overalls, wolf-skin pelisse, red cap with fur turn-up and cock's feather, blue cotton shirt, soft leather knee boots, buff sabretache and sky blue housings with a white fleur de lis. The hue of blue gradually darkened in the 1720s and various details changed. By 1735 the uniform was red dolman and breeches, blue pelisse, pewter buttons, white flat lace, fur cap with red bag, red cloak, black boots, reddish-brown leather belt and cartridge box and blue housings with orange fleur de lis. In 1739 it changed to blue dolman with red cuffs, blue breeches and cloak and brass buttons. The sky blue uniform ordered for hussars in October 1744 was not adopted by this regiment. Instead in 1747 they were reported as still wearing red dolman and breeches. In 1748 they wore a white mirleton cap edged with yellow lace, and in 1752 they were ordered into sky blue dolman, breeches and pelisse, pewter buttons, white cords, black fur edging the pelisse, and their regimental distinctive colour of yellow. However, it seems they continued to wear red dolman and breeches.

Bercheny: Formed from June 1720. Their early uniform was about the same as that of Rattsky. By 1735, the uniform was red dolman, blue breeches, blue pelisse, pewter buttons, white flat lace, fur cap with red bag, red cloak, black boots, reddish-brown leather belt and cartridge box and red housings with white fleur de lis. 1739: orange fleur de lis on housings. 1744: sky blue dolman, breeches and pelisse, red housings, probably white cords and pewter buttons. The hue of sky blue was darker in Bercheny than for other regiments. 1748: red mirleton cap edged with white lace. 1752: red cap and regimental distinctive colour of sky blue (but the dolman cuffs were red). Cap remained red in 1755 with sky blue wing and white lace edging. The officers in this regiment appear to have favoured red breeches instead of the regulation sky blue. From December 1762 the distinctive colour was red, and the green uniform was not taken into wear until 1768.

Esterhazy: Raised 1734/35. 1743 David. 1747 Turpin, 1761 Chamborant. Buff dolman and breeches, blue dolman cuffs, pewter buttons, white cords, blue pelisse, blue and white sash, black boots, fur cap with buff bag, blue cloak, red sabretache with the king's cypher at centre in blue and edged with blue lace, and buff housings bearing the king's cypher at the corner. From 1744: sky blue dolman, breeches and pelisse, red housings, probably white cords, and pewter buttons. 1748: white mirleton cap edged with black lace. 1752: regimental distinctive colour black.

Beausobre: Raised August 1743. Incorporated into Bercheny, Turpin and Polleresky from 30 October 1756. Early uniform unknown. From 1744, ordered to have sky blue dolman, breeches and pelisse, red housings. However, three years later they were not dressed according to regulation. 1748: white mirleton cap edged with false silver lace. 1752: cap as before but trimmed with blue, regimental distinctive colour blue.

Raugrave: Raised September 1743. Converted to heavy cavalry in 1756. Sky blue dolman, breeches and pelisse, red housings, probably white cords and pewter buttons. 1748: white mirleton cap edged with orange lace. 1752: regimental distinctive colour orange.

Polleresky: Raised December 1743. Disbanded in May 1758.[2] First dressed in 'cinnamon colour' by its colonel, who added green pelisses in 1744 or 1745, and changed it in c.1746 to sky blue dolman, breeches and pelisse, red housings, probably white cords, and pewter buttons. 1748: white mirleton cap edged with sky blue lace. 1752: regimental distinctive colour red.

Ferrari: Raised October 1745. Incorporated into Bercheny, Turpin and Polleresky from 30 October 1756. Sky blue dolman, breeches and pelisse, red housings, probably white cords, and pewter buttons. 1748: white mirleton cap edged with light green lace. 1752: regimental distinctive colour light green.

Du Chemin's corps, fusilier, 1735, by Gudenus.

Kleinholdt's corps, dragoon, 1735, by Gudenus.

---

2 This regiment was disbanded following reports by the Count of Clermont to the minister of war complaining of its bad discipline and looting, and this correspondance has often been used by historians. However, further study revealed that Clermont's reports were inaccurate and unfair. Colonel Polleresky's honour was eventually fully reinstated by the king. See La Sabretache, 1908, pp. 502-503.

Nassau-Saarbruck: Raised April 1756 as Volontaires. 1758 Royal-Nassau Hussars. Blue dolman with buff collar and cuffs and five rows of buttons, blue breeches, red pelisse edged with black fur, pewter buttons, white cords, ponceau red with orange and white sash, dolman cuffs, white cords, black cap with black wing edged with orange and white lace and white aigrette, red housings with orange lion and orange and white lace edge. From December 1762: orange facing colour.

Esterhazy: Raised February 1764. Regimental facing colour white.

LIGHT TROOPS

For most of Louis XV's reign, the organisation of light troops was almost individual to each corps. Some were independent companies, others were mixed legionary units with cavalry as well. Some were recruited from Frenchmen, especially in mountainous areas, but most were foreigners recruited from Germany, Austria, Flanders and the Balkans. The legionary corps were eventually amalgamated and reorganised into legions after the Seven Years War.

The strength of these units could vary a great deal. They were few in peacetime but their numbers would rise considerably in wartime. Towards the end of the War of Austrian Succession light corps amounted to 9,400 infantry and 4,750 cavalry. During the Seven Years War they totalled 7,800 infantry and 5,770 cavalry. From 1 March 1763 all legions were organised the same way: each had 460 officers and men divided into eight companies of dragoons, two grenadiers and eight of fusiliers.

Kleinholdt's corps, hussar, 1735, by Gudenus.

As will be seen below, the uniforms they wore were varied and often exotic. Hussar styles were prevalent in the cavalry formations from the 1740s, while brass neo-classical helmets became increasingly popular in the dragoon units.

Rank distinctions were generally the same in light troops as in the rest of the army. In 1759, for example, sergeants in the Volontaires-étrangers de Vignoles had silver lace edging or three silver laces on each cuff, the corporals had three wool laces and the *anspessades* had their cuffs edged with a wool lace.

Fusiliers de Montagnes: Companies of fusiliers raised from 1689 in Roussillon to serve in the Pyrenees as mountain troops. They were useless as garrison troops or in flat terrain, but were matchless as mountain patrols and as escorts to convoys. According to Chevalier de Guignard, who served with them, their dress was in the Miquelet style, consisting of a light blue-grey coat, blue cuffs and lining, red waistcoat, breeches of an unspecified colour. Their lower legs were often bare, and

Kleinholdt's corps, grenadier, 1735, by Gudenus.

they wore cord sandals and a blue wool cap called a 'Barretta'. They were armed with a pair of belt pistols carried on the right, a dagger on the left and a light Spanish-style musket called an 'escopetta', which they used so skilfully 'that they rarely missed their shot'. Instead of drums or trumpets they had horns made from a large sea shell which made 'an astonishing countryside sound'. These companies appear to have been embodied as needed for local duties from the late 17th century to about the 1740s, when the permanent corps of Fusiliers des Montagnes and the Volontaires Cantabres were raised (see below).

Klienholdt: Raised February 1719. Independent company of dragoons. In 1734 a fusilier company was added. 1741: dragoons became an independent company of Naudes and fusiliers became an independent company of La Haye in 1744. **1745: incorporated into Volontaires Royaux.** Coat, waistcoat and breeches entirely red, pewter buttons, silver hat lace with black cockade. From c.1734: dragoons wore a green coat, red cuffs, white lace, green waistcoat, buff breeches, pewter buttons, silver hat lace with black cockade, red housings laced white (1739: red waistcoat laced white). Fusiliers: blue coat, red cuffs, waistcoat and breeches, pewter buttons, white buttonhole lace, white lace edging waistcoat only, silver hat lace (Gudenus shows a mitre cap in 1735).

Arquebusiers du Roussillon: Raised in early 1719. Regiment of six battalions. Disbanded December 1722. Dressed in Miquelet fashion – 'earth grey or blue Gambette' (an ample full-bodied coat), blue lining, sleeveless waistcoat, breeches and stockings, brass buttons, false gold hat lace, a *baretille* (pointed wool cap). Officers had the same but the coat was 'earth grey' with 'blue or grey' lining, gold buttons and hat lace; no *baretille*. Regiment re-raised as four battalions in March 1734; disbanded February 1736.

Miquelets Espagnols: Regiment of six battalions raised in October 1719 from Spanish Catalan deserters. Probably short of recruits, it was disbanded in March 1720. Uniform unknown, but probably Miquelet-style.

La Croix's corps, hussar, 1735, by Gudenus.

Oge de Thiers: Raised February 1727. Independent company of fusiliers. Dragoon company added to corps 1734-36. **1737: Bock. 1745: incorporated into the Volontaires Royaux.** Fusiliers: grey-white coat and breeches, red cuffs and waistcoat, white stockings, pewter buttons and false silver lace. Dragoons: coat, waistcoat and breeches entirely red, pewter buttons, silver hat lace with black cockade, red housings laced white. From 1736: blue coat, red cuffs, waistcoat and breeches, pewter buttons, white buttonhole lace, silver hat lace.

Jacob: Raised February 1727. Independent company of fusiliers. 1735: dragoon company added to corps. **1745: incorporated into Volontaires Royaux.** Fusiliers: grey-white coat and breeches, red cuffs and waistcoat, white stockings, pewter buttons, false silver lace; from 1739, blue coat, red cuffs, waistcoat and breeches, pewter buttons, white buttonhole lace, silver hat lace. Dragoons: coat,

La Croix's corps, fusilier, 1735, by Gudenus.

waistcoat and breeches entirely red, pewter buttons, silver hat lace with black cockade, red housings laced white; from 1739, blue coat, red cuffs, waistcoat and breeches, pewter buttons, white buttonhole lace, silver hat lace, blue dragoon cap with red turn-up, blue housings laced white edged red.

Dulimont: Raised February 1727. Independent company of fusiliers. 1735: dragoon company added to corps. **1744: incorporated into the Arquebusiers de Grassins.** Grey-white coat and breeches, red cuffs and waistcoat, white stockings, pewter buttons, false silver lace. Dragoons: coat, waistcoat and breeches entirely red, pewter buttons, silver hat lace with black cockade, red housings laced white. From 1739: blue coat, red cuffs, waistcoat and breeches, pewter buttons, white buttonhole lace, silver hat lace.

Battenbourg: Raised February 1727. **1733 Edet, 1738 Montauban, 1741 La Harte.** Independent company of fusiliers. 1735: dragoon company added to corps. **1745: incorporated into Volontaires Royaux.** Grey-white coat and breeches, red cuffs and waistcoat, white stockings, pewter buttons, false silver lace. Dragoons: coat, waistcoat and breeches entirely red, pewter buttons, silver hat lace with black cockade, red housings laced white. From 1739, fusiliers had blue coat, red cuffs, waistcoat and breeches, pewter buttons, white buttonhole lace, silver hat lace; dragoons had blue coat, red cuffs, waistcoat and breeches, pewter buttons, white buttonhole lace, silver hat lace, blue housings laced white edged red.

Galhau: Raised February 1727. Independent company of fusiliers. 1735: dragoon company added to corps. **1745: incorporated into Volontaires Royaux.** Grey-white coat and breeches, red cuffs and waistcoat, white stockings, pewter buttons, false silver lace; dragoons: coat, waistcoat and breeches entirely red, pewter buttons, silver hat lace with black cockade, red housings laced white. Fusiliers shown by Gudenus in 1735 with blue coat, waistcoat and breeches, red cuffs and lining, pewter buttons, silver hat lace. From 1738, fusiliers: blue coat, red cuffs, waistcoat and breeches, pewter buttons, white buttonhole lace, silver hat lace; dragoons: blue coat, red cuffs, waistcoat and breeches, pewter buttons, white buttonhole lace, silver hat lace, blue housings laced white edged red.

Chateauvieux: Raised February 1727. **1733 Pauly.** Independent company of fusiliers. 1735/36: dragoon company added to corps. **1745: incorporated into Volontaires Royaux.** Fusiliers: grey-white coat and breeches, red cuffs and waistcoat, white stockings, pewter buttons, false silver lace. Dragoons: coat, waistcoat and breeches entirely red, pewter buttons, silver hat lace with black cockade, red housings laced white. From 1739: blue coat, red cuffs, waistcoat and breeches, pewter buttons, white buttonhole lace, silver hat lace.

Dumoulin: Raised February 1727. Independent company of dragoons. 1734-36: fusilier company added to corps. **1745: incorporated into Volontaires Royaux.** Coat, waistcoat and breeches entirely red, pewter buttons, silver hat lace with black cockade, red housings laced white. From 1738: red coat, green cuffs, lining and waistcoat, buff breeches, pewter buttons, silver hat lace.

La Croix: Raised February 1727. Independent company of dragoons. 1733: fusilier company added to corps. **1745: incorporated into Volontaires Royaux.** Dragoons: coat, waistcoat and breeches entirely red, pewter buttons, silver hat lace with black cockade, red housings laced white. Fusiliers shown by Gudenus in 1735 with blue coat and breeches, red cuffs and lining, pewter buttons (with buttons on each side of coat front), vertical cuff flap, red piping edging coat, cuff flap and pocket flap, red stitched buttonholes, red 'X's between buttonholes, silver hat lace. 1738: coat completely blue with white piping, buttonholes and 'X's, blue waistcoat and breeches, pewter buttons, silver hat lace. Dragoons: Gudenus shows these in hussar dress in 1735 with all-red dolman, white and crimson braid and sash, buff breeches, plain blue pelisse lined white, fur cap with red bag and white aigrette. 1738: dragoons reported wearing blue coat, red cuffs, lining and waistcoat, buff breeches, pewter button, silver hat lace, blue housings laced white and piped red.

Romberg's corps, dragoon, 1735, by Gudenus.

Gouverneur: Raised February 1727. Independent company of dragoons. **1733 Romberg. 1744: incorporated into the Arquebusiers de Grassin.** Coat, waistcoat and breeches entirely red, pewter buttons, silver hat lace with black cockade. 1739: blue coat, yellow cuffs, lining and waistcoat, pewter buttons, white buttonhole lace, silver hat lace.

Goderneaux: Raised February 1727. Independent company of dragoons. **1745: incorporated into the Volontaires Royaux.** Coat, waistcoat and breeches entirely red, pewter buttons, silver hat lace with black cockade. 1739: grey-blue coat, red cuffs, lining and waistcoat, buff breeches, brass buttons, gold hat lace, black cockade.

Le Noble: Raised December 1733. Independent company of fusiliers. **1735 Wandale. 1744: incorporated into the Arquebusiers de Grassin.** Grey-white coat, red cuffs. From c.1735: blue coat, cuffs, waistcoat and breeches, pewter buttons, silver hat lace.

Goderneaux's corps, dragoon, 1735, by Gudenus.

Provisy: Raised December 1733. Independent fusilier company. Disbanded 1736. Grey-white coat, red cuffs. 1735: blue coat, red cuffs, waistcoat and breeches, pewter buttons, silver hat lace. 1742: re-raised. **1745: incorporated into Volontaires Royaux.**

Independent Companies: Raised 1733 and 1734 and disbanded 1736. Each known by their captain's name. Fusiliers: **from 1733 – Le Blanc, Le Page; from 1734 – Béthune, La Tour, Digoine (from 1735 – Beaufort) and Boudet.** Dragoons: **from 1734 – Serette, Verkeim.** Uniforms were the same for all at first. Fusiliers: grey-white coat, red cuffs; however, from 1735 Le Blanc and Le Page changed to blue coat, red cuffs, waistcoat and breeches, pewter buttons, silver hat lace.

Dragoons: coat, waistcoat and breeches entirely red, pewter buttons, silver hat lace with black cockade, red housings laced white.

Duchemin: Raised June 1734. Independent company of fusiliers. **1745: incorporated into Volontaires Royaux.** Grey-white coat, red cuffs. 1739: blue coat (and probably breeches), red cuffs, buff waistcoat, pewter buttons, silver hat lace.

Arquebusiers d'Aygoin: Also termed 'Miquelets d'Aygoin', a 63-man company raised in February 1739 for service in Corsica. **December 1748: incorporated into the Fusiliers de Montagne.** Uniform unknown, but it is likely that they were armed and dressed in the Miquelet style.

Rochefort, Chevreau, Pantybock: Independent companies of dragoons. Raised 1741. They served in Bohemia, and apparently were dissolved after capture of Prague. Blue coat, red cuffs, waistcoat and breeches, hat laced silver with black cockade.

Fusiliers-Guides de Brück: 50-man company raised May 1741. **1745: incorporated into Volontaires Royaux.**

Pincheny: Raised early 1742. Independent company of dragoons. **1745: incorporated into Volontaires Royaux.**

Massanne: Raised December 1742. Independent company of fusiliers. **1745: incorporated into Volontaires Royaux.**

Du Bayet: Raised December 1742. Independent company of fusiliers. **1744: incorporated into Arquebusiers de Grassin.**

Bidache: Raised December 1742. One independent company of dragoons and one of fusiliers. **1745: incorporated into Volontaires Royaux.**

Volontaires de Saxe: Raised March 1743. Six 'brigades' each of 80 uhlans and 80 *pacolets* (dragoons). **1750 Volontaires de Friezen, 1755 Volontaires de Schomberg.** Converted to dragoons in December 1762. The uhlans had a green sweater-like upper garment and green trousers, Hungarian boots, brass helmet with a white turban criss-crossed with reddish brown leather straps. The mane of the helmet was in the colour of the respective brigades – white, yellow and so on. The uhlans of 1st brigade, whose colour was white, were recruited from free Blacks in France and acted as Marshal de Saxe's escort. They were mounted on white horses. The uhlans' weapons were a 2.9m lance with a pennant, a sabre and a belt pistol. Dragoons: green coat with red cuffs, collar, lapels and turnbacks, brass buttons, red wool aiguillette, buff leather waistcoat edged with red, leather breeches, dragoon gaiters fastening below the calf, brass helmet trimmed with seal fur and two brass rosettes, horse hair mane. Dragoons had a musket without a ramrod, bayonet always fixed, two pistols and a sabre. Wolf's hide housings. The 1762 Ms shows green turnbacks and white striped red lace edging the waistcoat.

Damiens: Raised September 1743. Independent company of fusiliers. **1745: incorporated into Volontaires Royaux.**

'Lafaire's' corps, dragoon, 1735, by Gudenus.

Chasseurs de Fischer: Raised November 1743. Initially 45 foot and 15 mounted chasseurs, much distinguished in action; then up to 400 foot and 200 mounted in September 1747. From 1756: 500 in four foot and four mounted companies. 1757: 1,200 men in eight mounted and eight infantry.

1761 Dragons-chasseurs de Conflans; 1763 Légion de Conflans. Disbanded 1776. Foot chasseurs: all green coat, waistcoat and breeches, plain hat with black cockade (this was a low green cap), black short boots, armed with rifled musket, bayonet and sabre. Mounted chasseurs: green hussar style dolman and breeches. 1744: red pelisse with grey fur, green dolman, brass buttons and yellow cords, red breeches, black cap with white plume, red housing

Galhau's corps, fusilier (right), 1735, by Gudenus.

with three fishes in yellow, armed with carbine, bayonet, sabre and pair of pistols. 1749: green pelisse. 1758: foot chasseurs wore green coat, cuff, lining, waistcoat and breeches, red collar, orange epaulettes, vertical pockets, brass buttons, green caps, bearskin caps for grenadiers; mounted chasseurs wore green dolman and pelisse, red small cuffs and breeches, brass buttons, orange cords, black hussar cap, red housings laced orange. The 1762 Ms shows red collar, cuffs, lapels and epaulettes for the foot, buttons set in pairs (but none on cuffs), bearskin cap with red bag and brass plate for grenadiers. 1763: foot chasseurs wore green collar and pointed cuffs with a button, no lapels and epaulettes, bearskin cap for grenadiers, hat laced yellow for fusiliers. 1765: mounted chasseurs officially became hussars, which they had been all along. Their uniform became completely green, pelisse, dolman and breeches, with yellow cords, black hussar cap lined and edged green, red sabretache edged with green lace piped yellow, white sheepskin housing edged green. 1767: foot chasseurs had green lapels, white breeches, black hat with yellow lace; mounted trumpeter of Conflan had red lined green, green waistcoat, multicoloured lace of yellow, white, red and green, pewter buttons, hat laced silver.

Arquebusiers de Grassin: Raised January 1744. Large corps of 1,300 men – 900 fusiliers in nine companies, 100 grenadiers in two companies and 300 cavalry in six companies. Augmented by 200 cavalry in May 1745. Reduced from 1,500 to 970 men in September 1748, to 640 in October and 340 in December. **August 1749: incorporated into the Volontaires de Flandres.** Blue short coat edged with white fur, black cuffs edged with white fur, red collar and waistcoat, brass buttons, blue breeches, grey gaiters, red hussar cap edged blue, brass plate, white plume, red and blue cockade. Armed with musket, bayonet and boarding sabre. The cavalry was equipped as hussars and its uniform was the same as the infantry except for an orange, blue and red aiguillette.

Le Noble's corps, fusilier, 1735, by Gudenus.

13

They had dragoon gaiters instead of boots, and each was armed with a carbine, two pistols and a sabre. Their cloak and housings were 'half-scarlet'. Officers had gold embroidered buttonholes.

Fusiliers-Guides du Dauphiné or de Tellemont: Company of guides raised January 1744 and disbanded December 1748.

Fusiliers de Montagnes: Raised February 1744. Battalion of 1,200 men in 24 companies, reduced to 720 men in 12 companies in February 1747. From December 1748 to its disbandment, in January 1763, the corps had only 120 men in three companies. These fusiliers wore a mixture of French uniforms and Miquelet traditional costume. Blue full-bodied coat and breeches, red collar, cuffs, lining and waistcoat, pewter buttons, silver hat lace, cord sandals with blue ribbons, blue cap with red turn-up laced white, blue apron edged red, also white linen baggy breeches. Armed with escopetta, bayonet and two pistols which were carried by a leather flap. However, in 1751, two out of three companies are reported armed with the standard infantry musket. The 1757 Ms shows the coat cuff edged with white lace and two buttonholes laced white and a double-breasted waistcoat. Officers were dressed French fashion in the same colours, without lace on the coat, and with silver buttons and hat lace.

Rosemberg: Raised April 1744. Independent company of hussars. **September 1748: incorporated into Nassau-Saarbruck cavalry.**

Zoller: Raised June 1744. Independent company of dragoons. **1745: incorporated into Volontaires Royaux.**

Gagneur: Raised July-August 1744. Independent company of fusiliers. **1745: incorporated into Volontaires Royaux.**

Volontaires Royaux: Raised August 1745. Initially 2,800 officers and men divided into two grenadier companies, one of pioneer-boatmen, one of guides, having each 125 fusiliers and 75 dragoons; reduced to 100 fusiliers in 1746. Outstanding services in Germany during Seven Years War. 1756: 950 men in 15 companies, two of grenadiers, one of pioneers (*ouvriers*), others each of 90 men, including 40 mounted. **1758: Légion Royale**, one company of hussars added. 1759: two companies of hussars. 1760: nine companies of infantry, including one of grenadiers, eight of dragoons. Disbanded 1776. Fusiliers: blue coat, red collar, cuffs, lining and waistcoat, buff or white breeches, pewter buttons on both sides of coat and waistcoat, silver hat lace, black cockade and cravat, white gaiters with black buttons and garters. Grenadiers: same but fur cap. Dragoons: same but white aiguillettes, blue cloaks, 'English-style' boots. Officers had ponceau-red velvet collar and cuffs, waistcoat laced silver, red breeches, hat laced silver with white plumes, silver aiguillettes. Drummers: king's livery with crosses on chest and back. 1750s: white breeches, bearskin caps for pioneers. Facings of officers seem to have become ordinary red. The 1762 Ms shows red lapels and shoulder straps for foot troops, blue dolman with red cuffs and blue pelisse with black fur, pewter buttons and black cords, red and black sash, red sabretache with white fleur de lis and edging for the

Captain Simon de Galhau, Galhau's Independent Dragoon Company, c.1740.

Jean-Chrétien Fischer, lieutenant-colonel commanding the Chasseurs de Fischer, c.1748. (Private collection)

LEFT **Chasseurs de Fisher, hussar, c.1747.** 'The uniform is a half-scarlet pelisse and lining edged with grey fur, yellow wool cords, green vest [dolman], yellow cords and sash, half-scarlet breeches, hussar boots, black cap, white plume and cockade, their weapons are a Hungarian style carbine, 2 pistols and a sabre and its scabbard trimmed with brass. The housings are red with three fishes in yellow wool.' (Print after de la Rue)

hussars. A dragoon shown by Becker at the same date has red lapels and would appear to be of this corps (see illustration on p.38). 1763: blue coat, lining and waistcoat (with red cuff flap), red collar and pointed cuffs with a button, pewter buttons, bearskin cap for grenadiers, hat laced white for fusiliers; steel helmet with brass crest and blue housing edged with white lace piped red for dragoons. 1767: red lapels and plain round cuffs, white lining and waistcoat; browned steel helmet with brass crest, red housings edged with white chain lace for dragoons.

La Morlière: Raised October 1745. 1,000 men divided into two companies of grenadiers, six of fusiliers and six of dragoons. Augmented in December 1746 to 1,500 men by adding three companies of fusiliers and four of dragoons. Reduced gradually in late 1748 to 340 men. **Incorporated into the Volontaires de Flandres in August 1749.** Fusiliers: brown coat, red collar, turnbacks, cuffs, waistcoat, breeches, red lace ending with fringes, pewter buttons, black hussar cap laced white; armed with musket, bayonet and steel-hilted sabre and steel scabbard. Grenadiers: same as fusiliers but with red lapels and no lace, bearskin cap with white cords and plume. Dragoons: coat same as fusiliers but with scarlet aiguillette, yellow waistcoat, buff leather breeches, steel helmet with red and black turban and three brass lilies in front; housing of white sheepskin edged yellow; armed with carbine, two pistols, steel-hilted sabre and steel scabbard.

Volontaires Cantabres: Raised December 1745. One battalion of 10 companies of 50 men each. Name altered to **Royal-Cantabres** in July 1747 and augmented to two grenadier companies, 16 of 75 fusiliers each, six companies of 50 hussars and an artillery detachment with two cannon. Reduced to four fusilier companies in 1749; expanded to a 604-man battalion in eight companies in July 1757 and nine companies, including one of grenadiers, in January 1759. Disbanded November 1762. Fusiliers: sky blue coat, crimson pointed cuffs, red lining, pewter buttons, white lace, white waistcoat, breeches and gaiters, crimson sash with white tassels, flat sky blue bonnet with white or white and crimson pompon, Spanish-style hair net. Grenadiers: cap with brass Prussian-style mitre, front stamped with a grenade and the royal arms, and sky blue back. Hussars: light blue jacket with crimson cuffs, pewter buttons, white lace, crimson sash with white tassel, buff breeches, hussar cap with a fleur de lis in front.

Fusiliers-Guides: Raised January 1746. Three officers and 25 men (12 mounted) as guides in Flanders Army. Disbanded 1748. Completely blue coat, waistcoat and breeches, pewter buttons, silver hat lace, housings blue laced white. Raised again December 1756 (same strength, same uniform) and disbanded 1763. Another company was raised in February 1761 as guides in the Lower Rhine Army (same strength, same uniform); disbanded 1763. The 1762 Ms mentions 200 foot and 60 dragoons. The foot

ABOVE **Volontaires de Saxe, uhlan, c.1747.** 'The uniform of the Uhlans is a green coat and trousers, Hungarian boots, brass helmet with a white turban criss-crossed with Russian leather straps, the mane of the helmet in the colour of their brigades, their weapons are a 9 feet lance with a pennant, a sabre and a belt pistol.' (Print after de la Rue)

ABOVE RIGHT **Volontaires de Saxe, dragoon, c.1747.** 'The uniform is a green coat, scarlet cuffs, collar, lapels and lining [or turnbacks], plain brass buttons, red wool aiguillette, buff leather waistcoat edged with scarlet, leather breeches, dragoon gaiters fastening below the calf, brass helmet trimmed with seal fur and 2 brass rosettes, the mane is of [horse] hair; their weapons are a musket without a ramrod, bayonet always fixed, 2 pistols and a sabre. The horse is covered with a wolf hide.' (Print after de la Rue)

had white buttonhole lace, the dragoons plain with black leather helmet with crest and turban with white lace set in zigzag, red sabretache with a crowned white wheel at the centre and two small white fleurs de lis.

Volontaires de Gantez: Raised January 1746 – 315 infantry, 144 hussars, 53 dragoons. **March 1749: incorporated into Volontaires du Dauphiné.** Blue coat, buff collar and waistcoat, buff leather breeches, short boots. Dragoons and hussars also in blue.

Croates Infanterie: Large Croat independent company. Raised May 1746 from deserters. 13 officers, 240 men. Disbanded 1748. Green dolman, red cuffs and collar, white cords, red hussar breeches, cloak and sash, black hussar cap with white plume and cockade. Armed with musket, bayonet, steel-hilted sabre; belt pistol worn on right.

Volontaires Bretons: Raised October 1746 – 1,060 fusiliers, 540 hussars. **August 1749: incorporated into Volontaires de Flandres.** Fusiliers: buff pelisse with blue cords, blue dolman, breeches and cloak, buff cuffs and cords, red and buff sash, black hussar cap edged with yellow lace and white aigrette; armed with musket, bayonet and brass-hilted sabre and brass scabbard. Hussars: same as fusiliers but black fur edging to pelisse, hussar boots, blue housing; armed with carbine, two pistols and brass-hilted sabre and brass scabbard.

Chasseurs de Sabattier: Raised February 1747. Two companies of 211 chasseurs each. Disbanded February 1749. Green coat, red collar, cuffs, waistcoat and breeches, brass buttons. Officers had gold piping edging their coat and waistcoat; sergeants had yellow lace; drummers had yellow 'brandebourg' lace and aiguillette.

Chasseurs de Béringhen: Raised February 1747. Two companies of

211 chasseurs each. Disbanded February 1749. Uniform same as Sabattier's.

Chasseurs de Colonne: Raised February 1747. Two companies of 211 chasseurs each. Disbanded February 1749. Uniform same as Sabattier's.

Volontaires de Lancize: Raised May 1747. One company of 211 chasseurs each. Disbanded February 1749. Uniform same as Sabattier's.

Volontaires de Belloy: Raised September 1747. Eight companies of fusiliers of 100 men each, one company of 50 hussars. **1748 de Bruelh**. Disbanded October 1748.

Volontaires de Geschray: Raised November 1747 – 400 dragoons and 800 infantry. Reorganised as Volontaires d'Alsace in February 1758. Six companies each of 30 dragoons and 40 infantry. Disbanded 1759. Blue coat, red cuffs, lapels and waistcoat, brass buttons, gold hat lace.

Volontaires de Velgra: Raised March 1748. 100 fusiliers and 25 hussars. Disbanded December 1748.

Volontaires du Dauphiné: Raised November 1748 – 210 men in five companies of fusiliers and two of dragoons. 1749: 120 men in five companies of fusilier and one of dragoons. 1758: eight companies each of 30 dragoons and 40 fusiliers. 1759: 948 men in eight companies of fusiliers, one of grenadiers and eight of dragoons. **March 1763: incorporated into the Légion de Flandre**. Fusiliers: blue coat, lining and breeches, buff collar, cuffs and waistcoat, pewter buttons, white buttonhole lace (lace on left side buttonholes of coat only), silver hat lace. Dragoons: same but white buttonholes on both sides of coat front, white epaulette, buff breeches, blue dragoon cap laced white with fur turn-up; blue housing laced white with dolphins. 1761: dragoons had brass helmet with brass crest, yellow leather turban and red plumes. The 1762 Ms shows all buttonholes with lace set in pairs, two vertical pockets with four buttons each, turban of helmet in brown fur.

Volontaires de Flandre: Raised August 1749. Three brigades each of 80 fusiliers and 40 dragoons from cadres of the Volontaires de Grassins, de la Morlière and Bretons. 1756: 12 companies, each of 40 fusiliers and 20 dragoons. 1757: six companies each of 70 men, including 30 dragoons. February 1758: eight companies of 75 men, each of 40 fusiliers and 35 dragoons. 1759: 948 men in eight companies of fusiliers, one of grenadiers and eight of dragoons. **March 1763 Légion de Flandre.** Disbanded 1776. Each of the three brigades of 1749 had a different uniform: 1st – buff coat, blue cuffs and waistcoat, pewter buttons; 2nd – blue coat, black cuffs, red waistcoat; 3rd – grey-black coat, red cuffs and waistcoat. 1756: blue coat, lining and waistcoat, red cuffs and lapels, white breeches, pewter buttons, white buttonhole lace, silver hat lace. The 1762 Ms shows a red collar edged white, red and white epaulettes, bearskin cap with red bag for grenadiers, black leather crested helmet with black mane and red turban with white criss-crossed ribbons. 1763: yellow coat and lining,

Marshal de Saxe in the uniform of a dragoon officer of his Volontaires de Saxe, c.1749. Note the gold epaulette. (Print after Liotard)

green collar, lapels and pointed cuffs with a button, yellow waistcoat with green cuff flaps, pewter buttons, bearskin cap for grenadiers, hat laced white for fusiliers, brass helmet for dragoons; housings of dragoons were yellow edged white. 1767: dark sky blue coat, white collar, plain round cuffs, lapels, lining, waistcoat and breeches, pewter buttons; white sheepskin housings edged sky blue, browned steel helmet with brass crest; sheepskin housings edged blue for dragoons.

Volontaires du Hainaut: Raised April 1757 by splitting the Volontaires de Flandres in two. Six companies each of 70 men, including 30 dragoons. February 1758: eight companies of 75 men – 40 fusiliers and 35 dragoons. **December 1762 Légion du Hainaut. 1768 Légion de Lorraine**. Disbanded 1776. Blue coat, lining and waistcoat, black collar, cuffs and lapels, white breeches, pewter buttons, white buttonhole lace, silver hat lace. The 1762 Ms shows for the dragoons white edging to the coat and waistcoat, blue pointed cuffs edged white, black leather crested helmet, black turban with white criss-crossed ribbons and no lapels for the infantry. 1763: blue coat, black collar, pointed cuffs and buttons, black epaulette, buff lining and waistcoat, white breeches, pewter buttons, white buttonhole lace, hat with white lace for fusiliers, bearskin cap for grenadiers; same for dragoons but buff breeches, black aiguillette, steel helmet with brass crest (with imitation panther fur turban and black mane), blue housings edged with white lace piped black. 1767: blue collar and lapels, black round cuffs with three buttons; browned steel helmet with brass crest: sheepskin housings edged blue for dragoons.

Volontaires Corses: Battalion raised April 1757. Served on the coast of Provence. Disbanded April 1760. Uniform unknown. During 1768/69 other companies of '*Volontaires Corses*' were organised by Colonel de Buttafuoco and fought with the French army against the Corsican '*patriotes*' following the cession of the island by the Republic of Genoa to France. Many subsequently joined Buttafuoco's Regiment (see Vol. 3) and the Légion Corse (see below).

Volontaires Étrangers de Clermont-Prince: Raised May 1758. 16 companies of cavalry, 11 of infantry, including two of grenadier companies. From 1759: same organisation as the Volontaires de Flandres. **1763 Légion de Clermont-Prince. 1766 Légion de Condé**. Disbanded 1776. Cavalry: buff coat and breeches, red collar, cuffs, lapels, lining and waistcoat, pewter buttons, white buttonhole lace on coat and waistcoat, brass helmet with red turban and white aigrette, buff cloak with red collar, armed with sabre, carbine and a pair of pistols. Infantry: same but no lapels, red aigrette for helmet of grenadiers (white for fusiliers); all armed with musket, bayonet and a hanger. 1763: no lapels, red epaulette for fusiliers; red aiguillette for dragoons, buff housings edged white with a red central stripes; bearskin cap for grenadiers, hat laced white for fusiliers. 1767: red lapels, white breeches for infantry, brass helmet with brass crest, buff breeches, sheepskin housings edged buff for dragoons.

Volontaires Liégeois: Raised August 1758. 600 men divided into four companies of cavalry, three companies of

ABOVE **Arquebusiers de Grassin, infantry, c.1747. 'The uniform is a blue coat, edged with white fur, black cuffs edged with the same, brass buttons, half-scarlet collar and waistcoat, blue breeches, grey linen gaiters, red cap edged with blue, brass plate in front, white plume, blue and red cockade; their weapons are a musket, bayonet and boarding sabre. (Print after de la Rue)**

The Chevalier de Grassin in the officer's uniform of his corps, the Arquebusiers de Grassin, 1744-49. Red hussar cap with blue wing embroidered with gold devices and white plume; blue coat with small red collar, black cuffs, white fur edging, red waistcoat and blue breeches; gold embroidery on coat and waistcoat, gold buttons, and blue sash with gold tassels. (Print after portrait attributed to Duplessis)

LEFT **Arquebusiers de Grassin, cavalry, c.1747.** 'The uniform is the same as the infantry except for an orange, blue and red aiguillette, dragoon gaiters; their weapons are a carbine, 2 pistols and a sabre. The cloak and housings are half scarlet.' (Print after de la Rue)

fusiliers and one of grenadiers. Disbanded October 1759. Red coat and lining, buff cuffs, collar, lapels, waistcoat and breeches, pewter buttons, white buttonhole lace. Dragoons had a brass helmet with red turban, black mane and white aigrette, red cloak, white sheepskin housing edged red. Fusiliers had a hat laced white, grenadiers a bearskin cap. The red uniform is according to French sources.[3] However, according to a plate showing the uniforms of the French infantry, which would have been made in 1759 for the Ms and was presented to King Carlos III of Spain in 1760 (now in the Royal Library at Madrid), the coat and breeches were blue and there are no lapels. Details in this plate, the only known contemporary rendering of this unit, are quite specific, suggesting that its author was well informed (see illustration).

Volontaires Étrangers de Vignoles: Organised in January 1759 from the remnants of the Volontaires-Étrangers (see Vol. 3); renamed in November 1759 **Volontaires d'Austrasie.** 948 men in one company of grenadiers, eight of fusiliers and eight of dragoons. **December 1762: incorporated into the Légion de Hainaut.** From 1759: blue coat and waistcoat, red cuffs, lapels and lining, white breeches, white buttons (seven on lapel and four below), white hat lace. All had short sabres. The 1762 Ms shows white buttonhole lace for foot troops; no lace and a black leather crested helmet for dragoons.

Volontaires de Cambefort: Raised December 1759. 50 dragoons and 100 fusiliers. Disbanded December 1762. Blue coat and waistcoat, red cuffs, lapels, lining and breeches, vertical pockets, pewter buttons, bearskin cap with red bag. Dragoons same with blue housings laced red.

Chasseurs de Sombreuil: Raised January 1760. Five companies, brigaded with Bercheny's Hussars. Became **Volontaires de Granpré** in 1761. Disbanded March 1761. Sky blue coat, red cuffs, lapels, lining, waistcoat and breeches, pewter buttons, white cord lace in a trefoil, white hat lace.

Chasseurs d'Origny: Raised January 1760. Five companies, brigaded with Turpin's Hussars. Disbanded March 1761. Sky blue coat, black cuffs and lapels, red lining, waistcoat and breeches, pewter buttons, white cord lace in a trefoil, white hat lace.

Volontaires de Saint-Victor: Raised February 1761. 948 men in one company of grenadiers, eight of fusiliers and eight of hussars. Incorporated into the Volontaires de Clermont-Prince in 1763. Blue coat and collar, red cuffs, lapels and lining, white waistcoat and breeches, pewter buttons, white hat lace. Hussars: buff dolman and breeches, red dolman cuffs and pelisse with brown fur, pewter buttons, white cords, red cap edged white with fur and yellow bag, buff housings edged white piped red. A contemporary painting shows the hussars with red dolman and breeches, buff dolman cuffs and pelisse. The 1762 Ms shows red waistcoat for the foot, and red sabretache with white fleur de lis and border.

---

3 Notably the order raising the corps and article by Rigo in La Figurine, No. 3, 1970.

ABOVE **Fusiliers de Montagne, c.1747.** 'The uniform is a blue casque [meaning an ample coat in this case], scarlet cuffs, collar, lining and waistcoat. Blue apron edged with red, very loose linen breeches, the espadrilles of foot wear are of cord laced with blue ribbon, hat edged with silver; their weapons are an escopette of 5 feet length, 2 pistols and a bayonet at the side.' (Print after de la Rue)

FAR RIGHT **La Morlière, dragoons, c.1747.** 'The uniform coat is the same as the fusiliers, adding only a half-scarlet aiguillette, yellow cloth waistcoat, leather breeches, dragoon gaiters, steel helmet having in front 3 brass fleurs de lis, scarlet turban with black leather [straps]; their weapons are a carbine, 2 pistols and a steel hilted sabre. The horse is covered by a sheepskin edged with yellow.' (Print after de la Rue)

Volontaires de Soubise: Raised February 1761. 948 men in eight companies of fusiliers, one of grenadiers and eight of dragoons. The 1762 Ms also mentions a chasseur company. **March 1763 Légion de Soubise**. Disbanded 1776. The order raising the corps mentions white 'Hungarian style vest' and breeches with white collar and lapels for the infantry, blue coat with blue collar and lapels for the dragoons. However, the infantry may have never adopted white since the 1762 register mentions these items as blue with white cuffs, lapels and cloak, pewter button on both sides of vest, no cords, black hussar cap edged white. Dragoons: blue coat and lapels, white cuffs (no buttons), lining, waistcoat and breeches, pewter buttons, white buttonhole lace, blue cap with fur trim, soft boots. For its part, the 1762 Ms shows the 'Hungarian style vest' as a blue coatee with short tails and no turnbacks, the buttonholes having white lace with a tassel, blue collar edged white, white epaulettes, bearskin cap for grenadiers. The same style is given for the chasseur company but green replaces blue. 1763: blue coat, white collar, pointed cuffs with a button, lining, waistcoat and breeches, pewter buttons, white epaulette, hat with white lace for fusiliers, bearskin cap for grenadiers. Dragoons had the same with white aiguillette, steel helmet with brass crest with imitation panther fur turban and black mane, blue housings edged white. 1767: white lapels, plain cuffs; bearskin cap for dragoons and sheepskin housings edged white for dragoons.

Volontaires de Poncet: Raised March 1761. 200 foot chasseurs. Disbanded March 1763. Green jacket and breeches, yellow cuffs and half lapels, pewter buttons, yellow gaiters, hat of 'approved' pattern, green cloak with yellow collar, armed with musket, bayonet and sword.

Volontaires de Monet: Raised March 1761. 60 foot chasseurs, 40 mounted chasseurs and 50 hussars. **December 1761 de Bonn. Renamed Volontaires du Quartier-Général in 1762**, having 500 men in four companies of foot chasseurs, four of mounted chasseurs and two of hussars. Disbanded December 1762. Green coat with green lapels and cuffs, green short waistcoat and breeches, green cap with wing lined white, armed with a rifled musket and a long knife-bayonet. Mounted chasseurs: green aiguillette, armed with sabre, pair of pistols and carbine. Hussars: green pelisse and dolman, white hussar breeches, green cords, armed with a sabre and a pair of pistols.

Volontaires Étrangers de Würmser: Raised January 1762. One company of grenadiers, eight of fusiliers and eight of dragoons. **Transferred to Austrian service in March 1763.** Green coat and waistcoat, black collar, cuffs, lapels and 'Hungarian' trousers, pewter buttons, black hussar cap, green cloak, black half-gaiters. Dragoons: green hussar dolman and waistcoat, black cuffs and breeches, white cords. The 1762 Ms calls the dragoons 'hussars'. They had all-black sabretache, black fur to pelisse, black cords, pewter buttons. The infantry coat is shown with a small black standing collar, no lapels, black pointed cuffs; buttons appear to be set in three rows of eight each, one at centre and one at each side, connected by narrow white lace or cord which also edged the top of the cuffs. Mixed white and black edging lace all around the collar, the front and the skirts of the coat and waistcoat.

ABOVE **Fusiliers de la Morlière, c.1747. 'The uniform is a brown coat, half-scarlet cuffs, collar, waistcoat and breeches, brande-bourgs [laces with tassels] of the same colour, black linen gaiters, black cap edged with white wool; their weapons are a musket, bayonet and a steel hilted sabre.'** (Print after de la Rue)

Légion Corse: Raised August 1769. One company of grenadiers, eight of fusiliers and eight of dragoons. Did not serve in Corsica. **Amalgamated with Royal-Corse Infantry Regiment in 1775 to form Légion du Dauphiné.** Disbanded 1776. Sky blue coat and collar, black cuffs, lapels and collar patch piped white, white lining, waistcoat and breeches, pewter buttons, black leather helmet with brown fur turban, brass badges and crest, black mane, red mane for grenadiers.

GENERALS, STAFF AND SPECIALIST OFFICERS

Until the 1740s generals and staff officers had no prescribed uniforms. They usually dressed in richly embroidered blue or red coats with plumed hats. In February 1744 the king and the minister of war determined that in the future generals should have a uniform when on campaign. This was a blue coat with blue cuffs and lining, with an elaborate gold embroidered broad lace edging the front, the pockets and the cuffs; the lieutenant-generals were to have a second lace on the cuffs and pockets, and gold buttons. With this, the generals tended to wear red waistcoats laced with gold, red or black velvet breeches, and a hat with gold lace and white plume edging. However, some generals tended to neglect wearing their uniforms, so in May 1758 the king reminded them to 'never stop wearing it' even for a single day on campaign. At the same time, the king authorised an undress coat which was the same as the dress coat but with the lace half as wide.[4]

Marshals were not assigned a specific uniform but tended, from the 1760s, to wear the same as generals with additional gold embroidery at the seams.

Staff officers and aides-de-camp of generals were ordered to wear a uniform on campaign in December 1756. It consisted of an all-blue coat with gold buttons and buttonhole lace (eight in front, two to each cuff, three to each pocket); for staff officers; plain all-blue coat, with gilt buttons for ADCs.

In November 1757 officers of garrison staff were also ordered to wear a uniform. Governors that had the rank of general continued to wear the 1744 general's uniform. Other garrison staff officers were to wear a blue coat with blue cuffs, red lining, gold lace buttonholes (both sides of the front, three per cuff and pocket) and gilt buttons – and there were various ways to lace the coat. Governors who did not have the rank of general officers had a 27mm gold edging lace with a second 22.5mm lace edging the coat in front, on the cuffs, pockets and back skirts. King's lieutenants, a rank equivalent to lieutenant-governor, had the 27mm edging lace and a second 40.6mm lace on the cuffs and pockets. Majors had only the 27mm edging lace. *Aide-majors* had no edging lace. Captains of the gates had the coat's front buttonholes on the left side only.

During the *Ancien Régime* many high-ranking officers – including princes, marshals, senior generals commanding armies and the

---

4 The Inspector General of Hussars, Count Bercheny, continued to wear his 'Hungarian suit' with royal permission from March 1744. But he also had the regular general's uniform to wear when not serving with his hussars.

ABOVE **Cantabres Volontaires, c.1747. 'The uniform is a sky blue coat, Polish [pointed] cuffs of crimson cloth, pewter buttons, white lace, linen gaiters, sky blue beret or cap with a white houpe [pompon], black net retaining the hair; their weapons are a musket, bayonet and a sabre and its scabbard garnished with whire brass.' (Print after de la Rue)**

governor-generals of provinces – were allowed their own bodyguard. The typical general's bodyguard unit consisted of a cavalry company of variable strength wearing the general's livery. Marshal Villar's guards, for instance, had a golden-brown uniform lined and cuffed with red or crimson and laced with silver. Between 1743 and 1750 Marshal de Saxe used the Volontaires de Saxe's first brigade of uhlans, recruited from Blacks, as his personal guards (see above). In 1744 the Prince of Conti's guards wore yellow with blue velvet cuffs, coat seams laced with silver, and blue bandoleers laced with silver. Marshal Mirepoix had two Swiss guards dressed in a grand livery of buff, with amaranth lace braided with silver, and bandoleers with fringes from which hung long rapiers; they wore a narrow tricorn with a plume. The Prince of Condé's guards had yellow coats with red cuffs.

Engineers

The 'King's Engineers' were not originally solely a military body. Its members were commissioned by the king to be in government service and could be employed designing civilian as well as military works. They had, in effect, their own ministry, which in the previous reign had been headed by Marshal Vauban himself – arguably one of history's most celebrated engineers. This brought them considerable independence from the army, the navy and provincial intendants for public works. Vauban's successor, the Marquis d'Asfeld, was not as famous but was a skilful courtier who managed to keep the engineers independent. On 10 March 1743, however, only three days following the death of the Duke d'Asfeld, the Ministry of War took over responsibility for fortifications and most of the engineers went to the army. However, the Ministry of the Navy integrated engineers devoted to coastal fortifications and those posted overseas in the various colonies.

The uniform of the 'King's Engineers' from 25 February 1732 was scarlet coat, lining, waistcoat, breeches and stockings, blue cuffs, gold buttons (four set in pairs on cuffs), gold hat lace and initially a white plume (though the latter is not mentioned after the late 1730s). Colonial engineers continued to wear this uniform until the end of the Seven Years War.

From 7 February 1744 the army engineers had a light grey-blue coat, likening, waistcoat and breeches, black cuffs, gold buttons, gold buttonhole lace and gold hat lace. On 8 December 1755 they adopted the same uniform as Royal-Artillerie – blue coat, red collar, cuffs, lining, waistcoat and breeches, gold buttons (three to each coat cuff and six to each pocket, two rows of buttons set in pairs on the waistcoat, three to each waistcoat pocket) and gold hat lace. When separated from the artillery on 5 May 1758, the army engineers were assigned a blue coat, black velvet cuffs, red lining, waistcoat and breeches, gold buttons (five to each cuff and pocket) and gold hat lace. Gold epaulettes were added in the 1760s but the coat remained single-breasted without lapels until 1776.

Administration officers and wagoners

The *commissaires des guerres* and the *commissaires-ordonateurs* were administration officers who saw to the army's supplies, finances, food, lodgings and so on. They held royal commissions and could have considerable

influence. Although under orders of senior officers when attached to armies, they were accountable to *intendants* – the senior administrative and police officials of French provinces. Indeed, in times of war the provincial intendants could also be *intendants des armées* having senior responsibility for military logistics and so on. These *officiers de plume* ('officers of the quill pen') initially had no uniforms but dressed as gentlemen and carried swords. From 27 March 1746 the *commissaires des guerres* were assigned a light grey-blue uniform with red cuffs and lining, and gold lace edging the coat; the *commissaires-ordonateurs* had two gold laces edging each cuff, the others a single lace.

At the other end of the scale were the civilian drivers of the supply wagons with the armies on campaign. During the War of Austrian Succession and the Seven Years War they were to have a uniform supplied by the contractors. It consisted of a white linen smock edged with blue lace, brass buttons (two in front, three under each cuff), a white linen dragoon-style forage cap with a white tassel at the end, blue turn-up edged with white lace and a white 'W' in front.

Medical services

Until the Seven Years War the medical officers had no prescribed uniforms. An unlaced grey civilian suit with a sword seems to have been their usual costume, some apparently also wore their regiment's uniform. By 1757 it was felt that a distinctive uniform was necessary so that medical officers be easily recognised during battles and in other circumstances where they were needed promptly. The following uniform was approved by the king on 15 July 1757: grey coat with red cuffs, waistcoat and breeches, and gold buttons. In the field hospitals surgeon-majors had their coats and waistcoats edged with a gold lace. Assistant surgeons had gold laced buttonholes, set one-two-three on the front, three to each cuff, pocket flaps and at each side of the back lower waist. Apprentices (or *garçons*) had no lace. Surgeon-majors at hospitals in cities or fortresses had the same uniform with gold buttons and laced buttonholes down the front, set evenly. Regimental surgeon-majors had the same uniform but with buttons set according to the regiment's fashion. The senior medical officers – the *médecins* – were only assigned a uniform (also grey) in 1775.

Hospitals in cities and fortresses were run by various religious orders, usually of nursing sisters but occasionally also friars. They wore the habits of their respective orders, as did the priests who visited to comfort patients.

Chaplains

In the French army, chaplains (called *aumoniers*) were attached to units. They had no specific uniforms or badges and wore the habits of their respective orders. Nearly all were of the Roman Catholic faith, but some foreign units – mostly Swiss – had Protestant chaplains for their Protestant soldiers.

ABOVE **Bretons Volontaires, fusiliers, c.1747. 'The uniform is a buff pelisse, blue cords, blue vest [dolman], buff cuffs and cords, sash of the same colour and red, blue breeches, black leather laced short boots, black cap edged with a yellow lace with a white aigrette; their weapons are a musket, bayonet and a sabre and its scabbard trimmed with brass.' (Print after de la Rue)**

FAR LEFT **Croate's Infanterie, c.1747. 'The uniform is a scarlet cloak, green vest [dolman], red cuffs, white cords, scarlet wool sash, Hungarian breeches of the same colour, black footwear, black cap, white plume and cockade; their weapons are a musket, bayonet, sabre garnished with white metal and a belt pistol worn on the right.' (Print after de la Rue)**

Cadets and military academies

The training of officers was the cause of some concern in Louis XV's army. Some were trained in the guard cavalry but the great majority had no formal training. The aspiring officers were often sons of officers and usually joined their regiment as cadets at a young age. They wore the regimental uniform, usually distinguished by an aiguillette of their unit's button colour, and were armed and equipped as private soldiers. Their schooling was basically the experience they gained in army camps and on campaign; certainly good practical training, but quite poor in terms of formal education and military doctrine.

A first attempt to correct this occurred in December 1726, when six companies, each of 100 cadets, were raised in various towns. This number was reduced to two companies in May 1729, and then to one in Metz in June 1732. Finally they were disbanded in 1733 when war broke out and the cadets were commissioned and sent to regiments. Their uniform was a blue coat with red cuffs, lining, waistcoat, breeches and stockings, brass buttons and gold hat lace.

In the late 1740s the king's *maîtresse en titre*, the Marquise de Pompadour, also became concerned about having a suitable military academy. Thanks to her influence, the king signed a decree, in January 1751, setting up the École Royale Militaire (Royal Military School) in Paris. The uniform was a blue coat and breeches, red collar, cuffs, lining and waistcoat, white stockings and black shoes, and silver buttons and hat lace. Some sources also indicate white lace edging the coat and facings. In 1763 this became red lapels, white waistcoat and breeches, with white lace edging the coat and facings. The best cadets – those in the 1st class – had a silver epaulette on the left shoulder; the 2nd class had a silver and ponceau red epaulette; the 3rd, red; and the 4th, brown.

At the beginning of the 18th century the professional training of engineers in France – then considered the leading country in military engineering – was still relatively informal. The object was to pass the stringent examinations that gave official recognition of a king's engineer. Only one in three hopefuls passed the exams. There were various private attempts to set up schools in St. Omer, Metz and Neuf-Brisach. Around 1737 or 1738 an engineer officer, the Chevalier de Lussan, founded the École de Mars in Paris, 'a sort of academy for the Art of War' which specialised in teaching 'everything that concerns the attack and defence' of fortresses. However, it closed about 1739 or 1740. Its cadets wore a 'red uniform with blue cuffs and a narrow gold cord' (Luynes' memoirs). Finally, in May 1748 the Ministry of War set up an engineer school at Mézières. It was designed to select the best candidates and train them to the highest scientific and military standards. The Mézières cadets wore the engineer uniform except for the gold laced buttonholes.

Bretons Volontaires, hussars, c.1747. 'The uniform is the same as the fusiliers, however the pelisse is edged with black fur, hussar boots, blue cloak and blue housings; their weapons are a rifled carbine, two pistols and a sabre and its scabbard trimmed with brass.' (Print after de la Rue)

HUSSARS 1710s-1740s
1: Esterhazy Regiment, hussar, 1735-43
2: Bercheny Regiment, officer, 1735

3: Bercheny Regiment, officer, 1720s
4: Verseilles Regiment, hussar, c.1716
5: Rattsky Regiment, c.1720

A

HUSSARS 1740s-50s

1: Raugrave Regiment, hussar, c.1752-56
2: Polleresky Regiment, hussar, c. 1744-46
3: Turpin Regiment, hussar, c.1757-60
4: Beausobre Regiment, hussar, 1752-56
5: Lyden Regiment, hussar, c.1745

B

LIGHT CORPS 1720s-40s
1: Fusilier or Miquelet des Montagnes, private
2: Arquebusier de Roussillon, private
3: Fusilier des Montagnes, private, 1740s
4: Kleinholdt, dragoon

4

1

2

3

LIGHT CORPS, 1740s-50s
1: Volontaires Breton, hussar, 1746-49
2: Volontaires de Geschray, fusilier, 1747-59
3: Volontaires du Dauphiné, fusilier, 1748-63
4: Le Noble, fusilier and officer, c.1734-44
5: Dumoulin, dragoon, 1738-45

D

LIGHT CORPS, SEVEN YEARS WAR
1: Volontaires de Hainaut, private, 1757-62
2: Volontaires de Soubise, chasseur, 1762-63
3: Volontaires-Étrangers de Clermont-Prince, dragoon, 1758-63
4: Volontaires de Saint-Victor, hussar, 1761-63
5: Volontaires de Flandres, dragoon, c.1762

E

GENERALS AND STAFF
1: Aide de camp, 1756-1774
2: Lieutenant-General, 1744-74
3: Maréchal de camp, 1744-74
4: Prince of Conti's Guards, trooper, 1740s
5: Commissaire ordonateur, 1760s
6: Commissaire des Guerres, 1746-74

F

ENGINEERS AND MEDICAL
1: Engineer officer, 1732-44
2: Engineer officer, 1744-55
3: Engineer officer, 1758-63
4: Apprentice, field hospital, 1757-74
6: Surgeon-Major, La Sarre Regiment, pre-1757

CONSTABULARY AND BOURGEOIS MILITIA

1: Maréchaussée de Lorraine et Barris,
   Trooper, c.1760
2: Maréchaussée de France, trooper, 1720-56
3: Cannonniers de Lille, 1720s

4: Stratsbourg Bougeois Militia, 2nd Cavalry
   Squadron, 1744
5: Metz Bourgeois Militia, Infantry, 1750s

3

4

5

1

2

H

From 1739 to 1766 the Duke of Lorraine and the King of Poland had a military academy of 48 cadets of noble birth – half were Poles and half were from Lorraine – led by 12 officers and organised as a mounted unit. They were instructed for three years in everything from history to dancing. Every two or three years 12 cadets were attached to French army regiments. The dress uniform was completely yellow, including the coat, waistcoat and breeches, with silver buttons, silver lace edging the coat and waistcoat, silver buttonhole lace on the coat and a silver laced hat. The brigadiers had silver embroidery edging their coats. The undress uniform consisted of a blue coat with scarlet Polish (pointed) cuffs and collar, gold buttons, scarlet waistcoat, breeches and stockings, and a gold laced hat.

CONSTABULARY CORPS

Matters concerning public order – such as the prevention of smuggling, the pursuit of deserters and stragglers, the escort of recruits and drafted militiamen, tax collection and a host of other duties – were, in the France of the *Ancien Régime*, the domain of special, military-like constabulary troops.

Archer corps had been raised in France during the Middle Ages to fight gangs of outlaws and in time they became units devoted to interior police and public order. Since they were under the authority of marshals, these units of archers became known as *Maréchaussée*. Eventually most

Altercation between two grenadiers of La Morlière's corps (left) and a member of Grassin's corps (right) involving a young woman, apparently in September 1746 near St. Pierre-sur-Meuse. (Anne S.K. Brown Military Collection, Brown University. Ph: R. Chartrand)

towns had a few 'archers' to perform local police duties. The name 'archer' was used for centuries after bows and arrows had disappeared since it came to mean 'constable'.

There were a host of other medieval names for various ranks. In 1769 some of the army cavalry rank equivalents were given: *prévôt-général* was colonel; *lieutenants* equalled army captains; *exempts* were lieutenants; brigadiers were *maréchal-des-logis*; *cavaliers* were brigadiers; and 'archers' were troopers or privates. The Maréchaussée units all had military duties and were considered part of the army; indeed, most were listed in the army registers.

Up to 1720 there were many varied groups of archers across the realm, but they were then grouped into the Maréchaussée de France, a national mounted constabulary corps. Its efficiency was even lauded in Diderot's *Encyclopédie*, which proclaimed, in 1751, that one could travel safely in all parts of France thanks to its patrols, and that 'there were less robberies in the kingdom of France in a year than there were around London in a week'. There were also several special units, as listed below.

Gardes de la Prévôté de l'Hôtel: Palace constabulary company of the royal guard. It had 100 men posted at Versailles and the Louvre, serving on foot and armed with swords and carbines. Its ceremonial dress consisted of a white silk cassock with elaborate gold embroidery of lilies and crowned 'L' which also included a 'Hercules' axe on the chest. The cassock's sleeves and skirt were red, white and blue with gold embroidery. The ordinary uniform was of the same colours as the Gardes de la Porte, but with gold lace and buttons (see Vol. 2).

Compagnie de la Connétablie: The senior company of the Maréchaussée, it was posted in Paris and acted as a guard for the senior marshal and the police archives. It often provided escorts for ambassadors and was also to 'prevent and stop fights between gentlemen and officers'. They wore a blue coat with red cuffs, edged with silver lace, and buttonholes and horizontal pockets edged with silver lace, silver buttons, red waistcoat, breeches and stockings, a hat laced silver with white plumes, and a buff belt edged silver. They were armed with a cavalry sword, pistols and carbine. In formal ceremonies they wore a blue cassock embroidered with gold and silver over their uniform. From December 1769 they wore a blue single-breasted coat with blue collar and cuffs, red turnbacks, waistcoat and breeches, white lace edging coat facings and buttonholes, white lace edging waistcoat, a hat laced silver with white cockade and plumes, and blue housing edged with white lace.

Maréchaussée de France: From 16 March 1720 there were some 30 mounted companies, one per province, amounting to 3,000 officers and men detached in a multitude of towns and villages. From 1720: blue coat with red cuffs and lining, silver lace edging the cuffs, white aiguillette, silver buttons, buff waistcoat and breeches, silver laced hat with black cockade, buff belt and bandoleer edged silver, black cravat, black dragoon gaiters with brass buckles, blue cloak with red cuffs, and blue housings laced white.

Volontaires de Dauphiné, 1757. (Musée de l'Armée, Paris)

They were armed with a cavalry sword, pistols and carbine. Each company had a trumpeter dressed in the king's livery garnished with silver lace.

Sous-brigadiers had three silver laces on the cuffs; brigadiers had three on the cuffs and three above on the lower sleeve; exempts had three on the cuffs, three on the pocket flaps and three in front of the coat; lieutenants had the same except for six laces in front of the coat set one-two-three from the collar and a silver aiguillette; the *prévôt* had the same but the laces in front were set in pairs, four on each cuff and pocket flap, and silver lace edging the waistcoat.

On 10 October 1756 important changes and additions were made. The aiguillette was abolished and replaced with silver laces in threes on the coat of the exempts and a silver lace edging the cuffs of brigadiers and sous-brigadiers. The bandoleer was no longer worn by brigadiers and sous-brigadiers. The troopers had the coat buttons set in threes and the coat cuffs each had six silver laced buttonholes. All were issued a blue surtout coat lined red with buttons set in threes – the exempts had all buttonholes in silver and the others had six white buttonhole laces on each cuff. The dragoon gaiters were replaced for all with black soft leather cavalry boots.

The next substantial changes came in a long regulation of December 1769 which introduced red collars and lapels to the coat, blue fleurs de lis on turnbacks. All buttonholes were to be laced, and white trefoil and aiguillette were brought back, as was the buff edged white bandoleer.

Compagnie du Prévôt Général de la Maréchaussée de l'Ille de France: This company policed the suburbs of Paris. They wore a blue coat with red cuffs, lining, waistcoat and breeches, gold buttons, gold lace edging cuffs, gold laced hat, buff belts edged silver, black dragoon gaiters, blue cloak, and blue housings laced gold. They were armed with a cavalry sword, pistols and carbine.

Compagnie de la Prévôté Générale des Monnaies: This company kept watch at the mint in Paris and escorted the transport of species. They wore an all-red coat edged with silver lace, silver buttons, silver aiguillette, red velvet bandoleer edged silver with a badge embroidered in gold and silver, yellow-buff waistcoat and breeches, heavy cavalry boots, and a hat edged in silver. They were armed with a cavalry sword, pistols and carbine. From December 1769: red coat with yellow collar, cuffs, lapels, waistcoat and breeches, white turnbacks, white lace edging facings and buttonholes.

Maréchaussée de Lorraine et du Barrois: Formed in October 1738 by the exiled King of Poland, who was Duke of Lorraine and the Barrois, it was 140-strong and existed until 1766, when it was incorporated into the French Maréchaussée. They wore a yellow coat with yellow lining and black 'Polish' (pointed) cuffs. Around 1760 the coat had a yellow collar and lapels with silver lace edging the

Fusiliers de Montagnes, 1757. (Musée de l'Armée, Paris)

Volontaires Cantabres, fusilier, 1757. (Musée de l'Armée, Paris)

collar, cuffs and lapels, a yellow waistcoat and breeches, pewter buttons, silver hat lace, and yellow housings edged with white lace.

Maréchaussée du Comtat: The Maréchaussée of this small, nominally papal, territory followed closely the organisation of its French counterpart, with detachments posted in Avignon, Cavaillon, Carpentas and so on. Its uniform was the same as the French Maréchaussée.

Prévôté de Dombes: The principality of Dombes, in southwestern France, had a small mounted '*prévôté*' of 14 officers and men, mostly posted in Trévoux. In 1727 its uniform was a red coat, blue cuffs edged with silver lace, blue lining, aiguillette of red, blue and yellow silk, blue waistcoat edged with silver, blue breeches, silver buttons, hat laced silver, black dragoon gaiters, buff bandoleer and belt edged silver, and red housings laced white. They were armed with a double-barrelled carbine, a bayonet, a pair of pistols, a pair of pocket pistols and a cavalry sabre.

Compagnies du Guet: The origin of these 'watch companies' goes back to the Middle Ages, when major towns hired armed men to keep the peace. By the 18th century, especially in Paris, these units were large, regimental-like corps, fully armed and uniformed.

The Compagnie d'Ordonnance du Guet, a Paris watch organised in 1666, became a legionary unit following large-scale riots in Paris during 1750. It was then reorganised, given military training and reinforced to 170 cavalry troopers and 472 infantrymen to patrol the city and 258 foot soldiers to guard the docks, gates and rampart. They were all armed,

Volontaires du Dauphiné, 1760.
Volontaires Étrangers de
Clermont-Prince, 1760. (Royal
Library, Madrid)

Volontaires de Flandres, 1760.
Volontaires du Hainaut, 1760.
Légion Royale, 1760. (Royal
Library, Madrid)

Volontaires d'Alsace, 1760.
Fusiliers de Montagnes, 1760.
Fusiliers-Guides, 1760. (Royal
Library, Madrid)

equipped and uniformed as regular cavalry and infantry. The cavalry had a blue coat and breeches, red cuffs and waistcoat, gold buttons and lace, and red housings laced gold. The infantry were 'dressed in blue, red cuffs and yellow buttons' with gaiters.

There had also been a Paris 'Compagnie du Guet', dating back to the Middle Ages, but by the 18th century its officers and archers had become corrupt and undisciplined. They wore all-blue coats with blue ban-

doleers speckled with yellow fleurs de lis. It was reorganised and further militarised in September 1771, when it numbered 78 officers and men. They wore a blue coat with blue collar, cuffs, lapels and lining, white waistcoat and breeches, pewter buttons, white epaulettes, and white hat lace; two silver epaulettes, buttons and lace for senior officers, one silver epaulette for junior officers and sergeants. The men carried muskets and bayonets, the sergeants halberds, and the officers batons on duty and spontoons on parade.

Other archer units, usually armed with swords, muskets and halberds, often in blue coats with bandoleers of fabric which might bear the city's coat of arms, had special duties. For instance, some cities had *archers de pauvres* (archers of the poor), who rounded up beggars and put them in hospitals. In 1718-20 there were other archers who tried to catch Paris prostitutes and other 'vagabonds' to ship them to Louisiana.

'A French Dragoon, 1762'
probably from the Légion Royale.
(Watercolour by C. Becker,
Weimar Library)

BOURGEOIS MILITIA

The *Milices Bourgeoises* were volunteer units raised in towns under local authority. They were usually recruited from middle class men who would thus be excused from paying some taxes, lodging troops and being enlisted in the royal or the coast guard militia. Many of these companies had ancient origins and might call themselves *arbalestriers* (cross-bowmen), archers and *arquebusiers*, while others called themselves *chevaliers* or *compagnie de l'oiseau* (bird company), which generally denoted a shooting club that used muskets. They were renowned for the lavish parades and dinners they organised. Others were less indulgent, but all units, whatever their name and standing, had watch duties. They usually provided the night patrols and, in towns with no garrisons, would stand guard and provide aid to civil power during riots – which occurred fairly frequently. The bourgeois militia could be mobilised when the enemy was near, as at Honfleur in 1758, or could take part in the defence of their city, as at Antibes in 1746.

It is hard to estimate the strength of these local forces, but they were obviously sizeable. The bourgeois militia of Bordeaux, for example, had around 6,000 men, Dunkerque had 4,200, Nantes had 3,000, Verdun about 1,000, Le Hâvre 900 and La Rochelle 400. In all, this must have amounted to hundreds of thousands of men who could be deployed for local service.

The Paris companies of arbalestriers, archers and arquebusiers, also known as the 'Garde de Paris' and the 'Gardes de l'Hôtel de Ville', originated in the 15th century. They were formed from merchants who, in return for their watch services, enjoyed various tax exemptions. Although militia, they were also considered part of the constabulary and ranked after the Maréchaussée. By the 18th century it was a 'posh' organisation, and it cost a couple of thousand pounds to become a member. The corps had 300 officers and men, 100 per company, until 1769, when a company of fusiliers was added and the companies were reorganised at 75 each.

From 29 December 1714 the Paris Guard uniform was an all-blue coat and waistcoat, silver buttons and buttonhole lace set in threes, red breeches and stockings, and a cassock bearing the arms of the king and of the city of Paris, armed with sword, musket and bayonet. From 7 October 1732: blue coat with red cuffs and lining edged 'everywhere' with gold lace, gold buttons set in pairs from neck to waist and four to each cuff and pocket, a red waistcoat without lace and with gold buttons in pairs, red breeches and stockings, gold laced hat with white plume edging, white leather gloves, a blue bandoleer edged with gold lace bearing two badges (one with the king's arms and the other the city's), and a sword with a gilt guard and silver wire grip with a red sword knot. From 11 April 1770: blue coat with red collar, cuffs, lapels, turnbacks, waistcoat, breeches and stockings, gold buttons and lace edging the facings of the coat, bastion-shaped lace at buttonholes, hat laced with gold with white cockade and white plume,

Légion de Flandres, dragoon, 1763-1766. (Painting by Edouard Détaille, Mr. and Mrs. Don Troiani collection, Southbury, CT)

white bandoleer edged and laced with gold with two plates (bearing the arms of the king and of the city). The mounted officers had red housings laced gold.

The *Canonniers Vétérans* of Lille were not really veteran gunners but a militia artillery association dating from the 15th century. The *Canonniers Vétérans* company, which had worn liveries in the 1480s, had no uniforms in the 18th century. Its men wore civilian coats and tricorns but carried muskets, swords and powder horns slung on a narrow shoulder belt.

In August 1717 some 57 companies of arquebusiers, mostly from towns in northeastern France, gathered at Meaux for a shooting competition and festivities. Many companies were dressed in uniforms, as follows: Noyons, red with silver buttonhole lace; Condé and Bar-sur-Seine, grey-blue with silver buttons; Châlons-sur-Marne and Peronne, grey with silver buttons; Nogent-sur-Seine, grey with silver buttons and blue cockade; Vertus, St. Dizier and Dormans all had grey with silver buttons; Soissons, red with silver lace; Laon and Mondidier, red with silver buttons; Troyes, brown with silver lace and buttons; Neuilly, La Ferté-Gaucher and Tours, brown with silver buttons; Brie, grey-white with silver buttons and blue cockades; Reims and Vailly, red; Coulommiers, red with gold buttons; Meaux, grey laced silver; Corbeil, Mantes and Épernay, grey; Provins, grey with silver buttonholes and pink cockades; La Ferté-sous-Jouare, olive; Fisme, maroon; La Ferté-Miton, Melun and St. Menehould, maroon with silver buttons; Torrigny, grey-blue with the marksman in red and blue; Poissy and Fer-en-Tardenois, brown; Beaumont and Bar-sur-Aube, cinnamon; Avenay, musk; and Guignes, grey-white with silver buttons.

Legions, hussars and troops in the French Army, 1767. (Private collection. Photo courtesy A.U. Koch)

In 1719 Cambrai had a company of arbalestriers in scarlet with gold cloth cuffs and waistcoat, gold buttons and lace. The archers and cannoneer companies wore blue laced with gold.

In 1720 the Nantes bourgeois militia's commanding officer wore a red coat with gorget and spontoon. A grey-white coat with blue cuffs, lining, waistcoat, breeches and stockings, and silver buttons and hat lace was later adopted by the Nantes militia who in 1733 were also ordered to wear swords.

In 1721 the four companies of the Marseille militia paraded wearing ribbons 'of the colours of the city' on their hats.

In 1722 the Troyes arquebusiers adopted a scarlet coat with black velvet cuffs and collar, gold buttons, yellow waistcoat and breeches, white silk stockings, white cravat, hat with white plume edging and white cockade, and a white silk shoulder sword-belt with a gold fringe. In the 1750s it was a red coat and breeches, white waistcoat, gold buttons, and a hat laced gold with white plumes.

In 1723 Reims had a bourgeois cavalry troop of 40 men who wore blue cassocks edged with white.

Chartres had a *compagnie de l'oiseau royal* (royal bird company), organised in April 1724, who wore a grey coat lined red and edged with silver lace, silver buttons, red stockings and silver hat lace.

In 1729 the two companies in Montpelier adopted a brown uniform: the married men's company uniform was lined with brown and edged with silver lace; the young bachelors' had brown with blue satin cuffs, lining and waistcoat, the waistcoat being laced.

The town of Mantes organised four companies of bourgeois militia in 1730. They were dressed in white with blue, red, green or yellow facings – one colour per company.

Montargis also had its *compagnie de l'oiseau* during the 1730s, in blue coat, red cuffs, waistcoat and breeches, and gold buttons and buttonhole lace. The companies of arbalestriers and of grenadiers had a white coat with red lapels and a beaver fur cap with a plate bearing the city's coat of arms. Officers had red coats with blue cuffs and gold buttons. Drummers wore the Orléans livery.

Companies of arquebusiers in the province of Champagne during the 1740s and 1750s had, at Châlon-sur-Marne, blue coat and breeches, red cuffs and waistcoat, silver buttons and buttonhole lace, and a hat laced silver. The Reims company had the same but with gold buttons and lace.

The *cinquantiers* of Abbeville had, in the 1740s, a blue coat and breeches, red collar, cuffs, lining, waistcoat and stockings, gold buttons, buttonhole lace and hat lace.

Lunneville in Lorraine had, in 1744, two mounted companies of bourgeois militia dressed in green.

The militia of Pontivy in Brittany had, from 1744, an all-white coat with white collar lined red, gilt buttons set in pairs, and a hat laced gold. Drummers and fifers were dressed by the Duke of Rohan, no doubt in his livery.

Légion Corse, officer, c.1769-75. (Print after miniature)

Stratsbourg had a large militia which, in 1744, was all in uniform for the king's visit. The hussar company was in scarlet with silver buttons and cords, bearskin cap with blue bag piped silver, and blue housings laced silver. The cavalry's 1st squadron had a red coat and waistcoat, black velvet collar, gold buttons and lace edging the coat and waistcoat, a hat with gold lace and white plume edging, and red housings laced gold. The 2nd squadron had the same dress but with silver buttons and lace. The 3rd squadron had a blue coat with black velvet collar, buff waistcoat, silver buttons and lace edging the coat and waistcoat, hat with silver lace and white plume edging, and scarlet housings laced silver. The 4th squadron had an ash grey coat with black velvet collar, buff waistcoat, silver buttons and lace edging the coat and waistcoat, a hat with silver lace and white plume edging, and scarlet housings laced silver. The first corps, consisting of five infantry companies, had a blue coat and breeches, red waistcoat, gold buttons and buttonhole and lace, gold hat lace; the grenadiers had a bearskin cap and a scarlet bag with a silver and red grenade embroidered in front. The second corps of three infantry companies had an all-scarlet uniform with gold buttons and buttonholes, and the grenadiers had a bearskin cap with scarlet bag piped gold, with a gold grenade embroidered on the front. Finally, a corps of two companies of *ouvriers* (artisans) had a pearl grey coat with black velvet collar, a brown waistcoat, and silver buttons and lace.

In 1749 Le Havre had a company of cavalry wearing a blue coat and breeches, crimson collar, cuffs and waistcoat, gold buttons and lace, and a gold-laced hat with white plume and cockade; the bourgeois militia officers had a red uniform with blue cuffs.

The militia officers of the 12 companies in Rouen had, in

Lieutenant-general Pierre de Rigaud, Marquis de Vaudreuil, c.1755. (National Archives of Canada, C3708)

A town major in the middle of the 18th century. (Anne S.K. Brown Military Collection, Brown University. Ph: R. Chartrand)

1749, scarlet coats with silver silk cuffs, white waistcoat laced gold, red breeches and white stockings.

The 80 militia dragoons of the town of Gap had, from the 1750s, scarlet coats with green cuffs, white turnbacks, waistcoat and breeches, black boots and tricorns.

Metz had four battalions of bourgeois militia during the 1750s. Their uniform was a blue coat with red collar, cuffs and lining, gold buttons and gold laced buttonholes, scarlet waistcoat laced gold, scarlet breeches, gold laced hat.

Soissons had a 'Compagnie Militaire' recruited in the bourgeoisie from 1753, wearing a blue uniform with white collar and lapels.

The Corbeil Compagnie de l'Arquebuse Royale wore, from 1757, a light grey-blue coat cuffed and lined with the same colour, crimson waistcoat and breeches, gold buttons and buttonhole lace on coat and waistcoat, white stockings and gloves, black cravat, a hat laced gold with white plume and edging, and a green and white cockade.

In 1757, fearing a British raid, the militiamen of La Rochelle mobilised into four fusilier companies named Volontaires d'Aunis. Their uniform was white coat, lining and breeches, red cuffs and waistcoat, brass buttons, gold hat lace – the same as the regular Aunis regiment. The city also had: Volontaires de Langeron, in blue coat with gold epaulette on the left shoulder, scarlet cuffs, waistcoat and breeches, brass buttons, hat laced gold, with blue and white cockade; Bonaventure's company, in grey-blue coat, black velvet cuffs, red waistcoat and breeches, and white cockade; the Mayor's company, in blue coat, red cuffs, waistcoat and breeches, gold and silk epaulette, white and red cockade; and two companies of *grenadiers bourgeois*, in white coat, red cuffs, waistcoat and breeches, and a grenadier bearskin cap with a brass plate stamped with the royal arms.

In October 1758 the Volontaires du Comte de Grammond were raised in Bayonne – 100 officers and men. They were apparently disbanded in 1762. Their uniform was a yellow coat with red cuffs, waistcoat and breeches, a bearskin cap with a yellow bag and low black laced boots instead of gaiters. Officers and men were armed with a musket, bayonet, sabre and a 20-round cartridge box. The two drummers, the fifer and the tambourine player would also have had yellow and red uniforms, as this was the Grammond livery, with red and blue lace on all seams, and yellow drums with the count's arms.

Bordeaux had several volunteer companies, one of which was the Volontaires d'Egmont – 67 officers and men raised about 1759 by the Countess d'Egmont. She would lead her volunteers in uniform, sword in hand, during parades, while they sang her glory to the popular tune *Belle Brune que J'adore* (Lovely Brunette that I Adore). Their uniform was red with black velvet cuffs, silver aiguillette, and white plumes and cockade.

In the province of Roussillon was a peculiar bourgeois militia called Soumettans (or *Soumatenès* in the local dialect) which was mobilised to garrison fortified towns. A 1762 register of Roussillon showed its uniform to have been in the style of the Fusiliers de Montagne: blue sleeved waistcoat, linen breeches, a blue cap with white lace border and tuft, with a red edged white turn-up at the front, and hair tucked in a hairnet. They were armed with an escopetta with bayonet, a belt pistol, a powder flask and a ventral cartridge box.

The captains of the Orléans militia had, in 1763, red uniforms; the drummers wore the livery of the Duke of Orléans.

The Dijon militiamen patrolling the streets first had civilian dress but were armed and the officers had gorgets. In 1765 the watch detachments adopted a red coat with buff collar, lapels, waistcoat and breeches, and silver hat lace.

SELECT BIBLIOGRAPHY

Delaunay, L.A., *Étude sur les Anciennes Compagnies d'Archers, d'Arbalestriers et d'Arquebusiers*, Paris 1879

'Les Hussards Français de l'Ancien Régime', *La Sabretache*, Special 1970

de Marbot, Alfred, & Dunoyer de Noirmont, *Costumes Militaires Français*, Paris 1846

de Prat, Olivier, *Médecins Militaires d'Autrefois*, Paris 1935

Sapin-Lignières, Armand, *Les Troupes Légères de l'Ancien Régime*, Saint-Julien-du-Sault 1979

Vanson, Louis, 'Le Premier Uniforme des Officiers Généraux' and 'Archives des Hussards', *Carnet de la Sabretache*, 1894 and 1898

Many descriptions of the bourgeois militia were found in histories of cities and provinces.

Collections of royal orders at the Service Historique de l'Armée de Terre, Château de Vincennes, at the Musée de l'Armée in Aix-en-Provence, and at the Anne S.K. Brown Military Collection, Brown University Library, Providence, USA.

General officers and staff, 1767. (Private collection. Photo courtesy A.U. Koch)

THE PLATES

HUSSARS 1710-1740s

A1: Esterhazy Regiment, hussar, 1735-43 Ordered raised in December and formed from 25 January 1735 in Stratsbourg, the regiment – raised to six squadrons – took part in the capture of Prague in 1741. Back in France, it became David's Regiment two years later. The first regiment to have a uniform which was not the traditional sky blue worn by hussars in French service until then, Colonel Esterhazy selected a distinctive buff dress which the regiment wore until it changed colonel in 1743 and took sky blue the following year.

A2: Bercheny Regiment, officer, 1735 The regiment campaigned in Germany during the Polish Succession War of 1733-35, including at the siege of Philipsbourg, where Gudenus sketched one of the regiment's hussars. As can be seen by comparing with figures A3, A4 and A5, the dress of these hussars was more polished and sophisticated than in previous decades.

A3: Bercheny Regiment, officer, 1720s Early hussar officers often had their own ideas about what constituted uniform dress. For instance, red breeches seemed better to some of Bercheny's officers, and were seen right up to the end of the Seven Years' War. Yet another example that Louis XV's

Maréchaussée de France, trooper, c.1770-75.
(Anne S.K. Brown Military Collection, Brown University.
Ph: R. Chartrand)

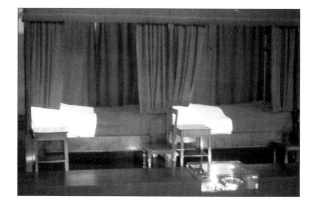

In the 18th century, the better hospital wards where seriously wounded officers, and sometimes enlisted men, were treated often featured rows of beds such as these preserved examples at the Hospices de Beaune in Burgundy, each with a chair and a small table. The bed covers and curtains were usually of dark red or green material. French hospitals were nearly always run by religious communities of nuns who provided the nursing and administrative staff.

hussars took dress regulations as suggestions rather than as orders: the original recruits for this hussar regiment came to Provence from Istanbul during the winter of 1719/20. In time, as in other hussar regiments, they became increasingly French, attracted by French ways and dress styles.

A4: Verseilles Regiment, hussar, c.1716 Raised as Kroneberg's in 1692, this was the first hussar regiment in the French army. Its companies were dispersed in other foreign cavalry units in 1698 but it was reconstituted as Verseilles' in 1705. It gave good service but was ordered incorporated into Rattsky's in May 1716. Leaving Metz very bitter, the men mutinied on the way to be incorporated at Verdun, and the corps dissolved. Its uniform and the style of the men was typical of early hussars, who cultivated a fierce, wild and rather oriental appearance.

A5: Rattsky Regiment, hussar, c.1720 This unit took part in the short half-hearted war against Spain in 1719/20 with the French army that campaigned in northern Catalonia. Their style was still very wild 'Hungarian', as this figure, based on a watercolour by Delaistre, shows.

HUSSARS 1740s-1750s

B1: Raugrave Regiment, hussar, c.1752-56 Raised in 1743 by the Count of Raugrave, the unit saw much action in the major battles and sieges of the Austrian Succession War in Flanders. The regiment is first mentioned with its distinctive orange (*aurore*) trim on the cap in 1748 (by 1752 they had orange cuffs too), but this colour may have been used before it was actually mentioned in orders. In any event, the hussar dress was worn until 1756, when the regiment was converted into heavy cavalry and renamed Volontaires Liégeois (see MAA 296, *Louis XV's Army (1) Cavalry & Dragoons*).

B2: Polleresky Regiment, hussar, c.1744-46 The first uniform of this unit was cinnamon coloured with green pelisses. Few other details are known, but the cords were probably white. This was a far cry from the official sky blue uniform which the regiment seems to have adopted towards the end of the War of Austrian Succession.

B3: Turpin Regiment, hussar, c.1757-60 This figure, based on a drawing by Christian Becker, is another example of relative uniformity in hussar regiments – its uniform is mostly red when it was supposed to be sky blue with black. It seems that the squadrons from Lynden's regiment amalgamated into Turpin's in 1756 continued to wear their uniform.

B4: Beausobre Regiment, hussar, 1752-56 Raised in 1743 by the baron of Beausobre, it was deployed in Flanders, taking part in many battles including Fontenoy and the sieges of Tournai, Berg op Zoom and Maestricht.

B5: Lynden Regiment, hussar, c.1745 The count of Lynden succeeded Colonel Rattky in 1743 and, under his command, Lynden's was participated in many engagements during the War of Austrian Succession including the battles of Fontenoy and Lawfeld. This figure, which gives a good idea of the evolution in style by the 1740s, is based on a drawing by Lenfant.

LIGHT CORPS 1720s-1740s

C1: Fusiliers, or Miquelets des Montagnes, private This figure is based on an engraving in Chevalier de Guignard's École de Mars, published in 1725, which also described companies who were most effective in the mountains of Roussillon. Each company had a 'bugler' using a sea shell as a horn for signals. The peculiar arms, equipment and dress were typical of the mountaineers of the Pyrenees.

C2: Arquebusiers du Roussillon, private This large multi-battalion regiment mobilised mountaineers in 1719-22 and 1734-36 and fought against the Spanish at mountain forts and passes. It was dressed in a Miquelet-style 'uniform' of sorts, with many variations. In a January 1719 order, the uniform was grey-white except for in Delio's battalion, which was to have the uniform of the war – blue lined red. But in March the dress was supposed be brown. However, a clothing bill of 1719 featured the following: 'earth grey' lined with blue, blue waistcoat, breeches and stockings, brass buttons, hat laced with false gold, and a barretine cap.

C3: Fusilier des Montagnes, private, 1740s This more permanent unit existed from 1744 to 1763. Its dress was a mixture of standard uniform and regional costume. A private could be wearing a standard tricorn, a barretine cap or, as shown here, a berrette – a large flat bonnet.

C4: Kleinholdt, dragoon, c.1719-39 This was one of the early light corps raised in Louis XV's reign. The trooper has

Arquebusiers from various bourgeois militia companies from northern France gathered at Maux in August 1717 for several days of shooting competitions, parades and elaborate banquets, the usual activities when the companies assembled. (Print after Desjardins)

the all-red uniform worn until about 1734. The Chevalier de Kleinholdt was an experienced officer who led his men in many successful skirmishes during 1733-35.

LIGHT CORPS 1730s-1750s

D1: Volontaires Breton, hussar, 1746-49 There is something quaint about this unit of 'volunteers of Brittany' dressed as hussars, both the horse and foot troops. While there were recruits from various places, the majority of the corps was composed of men from Brittany, some of whom were described as having a 'loose morality' but made very good soldiers. Sent into Flanders in 1747, they were heavily engaged at the siege and capture of Berg-op-Zoom in September, suffering heavy casualties including the loss of their commander, Colonel de Kermellec, which the king himself expressed regret over. The following year the Bretons were with Marshal de Saxe's army when it captured Maestricht.

D2: Volontaires de Geschray, fusilier, 1747-59 Raised in the later part of the Austrian Succession War by Jean Michel Geschray and recruited from Germans, the corps was deployed in 1748 with the French army near the Meuse. Reduced to only 120 men in peacetime, Geschray's establishment was multiplied tenfold with the outbreak of the Seven Years War. Geschray himself deserted to the Prussians following the French disaster at Rossbach in 1757, but the corps, which was then put under the command of Colonel de Beyerlé, served with French forces in the Lower Rhine as the Volontaires d'Alsace until disbanded in 1759.

D3: Volontaires du Dauphiné, fusilier, 1748-63 This unit was created at the end of the Austrian Succession War to amalgamate and retain the cadres of various light corps. Its first campaign was with Marshal Contades' army, which was beaten at Minden in 1758. Transferred to the Lower Rhine, the corps' good conduct contributed to the French success at Korback in July 1760. The following years saw further successes in engagements in Germany.

D4: Le Noble, fusilier private and officer, c.1735-44 Le Noble's light corps was raised at the beginning of the Polish Succession War, in 1733, and was deployed in the Philipsbourg area. The corps became Wandale's in early 1735. During the War of Austrian Succession it formed part of the French army in Westphalia until amalgamated into the Arquebusiers de Grassin in 1744. First clad in grey-white, it soon changed to a blue uniform.

D5: Dumoulin, dragoon, 1738-45 The chevalier Dumoulin was an experienced and renowned commander of light troops when he was among those selected to raise a dragoon company in 1727 and a fusilier company in 1734. During the War of Spanish Succession Dumoulin had beaten a body of British cavalry, taking its standards and kettledrums. These were carried by the new corps. In January 1735 the corps captured a body of enemy hussars near Philipsbourg. The dragoons first had an all-red uniform but green facings were added around 1738, while they were posted at Sarrelouis. It campaigned in Germany at the beginning of the War of Austrian Succession. In 1743 Dumoulin retired, taking the British trophies with him to decorate his manor. Command passed to the Count of Limoges, but the unit was incorporated into the Volontaires Royaux in 1745.

LIGHT CORPS, SEVEN YEARS WAR

E1: Volontaires de Hainaut, private, 1757-62 This unit saw much distinguished action during the Seven Years War. The corps first saw action at Haastembeck in 1757, then participated in the surprise attack on Harbourg, where it captured hundreds of enemy soldiers and several flags but surrendered with the rest of the garrison of Minden in March 1758 after a stubborn resistance. Re-raised by a new commander, Thomas-Auguste de Grandmaison (author of *La Petite Guerre*, a book on partisan warfare), the corps was again deployed in Germany to fight at Bork, Minden, Mardorf, Nordecken and Laughaus during 1759, rescued Bercheny's hussars in a skirmish during July 1760 and captured Minden in August. Perhaps its most outstanding feat occurred in August 1761, when it captured the infantry of Geschray's Prussian Free Corps at Nordhausen.

E2: Volontaires de Soubise, chasseur, 1762-63 The chasseur company is shown in the 1762 Ms in a green uniform, although the dragoons and grenadiers had blue, but all had the white facings and trim. The chasseurs were probably armed with a hanger and a short musket. The Prince of Soubise paid to raise the corps, which departed Quesnoy in March 1761 to campaign in Germany. Soubise's

Garde de Paris, private, 1770. The four companies of this corps were a combination of bourgeois militia and police force. This print shows the ornate uniform worn from 1770: blue coat with red collar, cuffs, lapels, turnbacks, breeches and stockings, gold buttons and lace, hat laced with gold with white cockade and white plume, white bandoleer edged and laced with gold. (*Recueil des chartes ...des ...arbalestriers, archers, arquebusiers et fusiliers de la ville de Paris*, Paris, 1770)

corps was successful in small engagements in August, putting to good use their two Rostaing guns, and again in 1762, at the battles of Asfeld and Zeigenheim. The corps initially had guidons and colours, but these were withdrawn in the reorganisation into a legion in 1763.

E3: Volontaires Étrangers de Clermont-Prince, dragoon trooper, 1758-63 The Count of Clermont raised this volunteer corps, which was soon deployed in Germany. With Fischer's corps they captured two enemy standards in a February 1759 engagement, but their luck turned when part of the corps, and many of its officers, were literally caught asleep at Zeirenberg in September 1760. Their dress was very distinctive, consisting of a buffish yellow coat with red facings and a brass helmet.

E4: Volontaire de Saint-Victor, hussar, 1761-63 The dress of the hussars is usually given as buff with red pelisse, but it seems that there was another dress. Our figure, based on a painting in a private collection, shows a very attractive red uniform with buff pelisse and dolman cuffs. The corps distinguished itself as scouts for Marshal Broglie's army deployed in western Germany and was involved in several skirmishes.

E5: Volontaires de Flandres, dragoon, c.1762 Formed in 1749, this corps was renowned for its good conduct and, deployed in Germany in the last years of the Seven Years War, participated in several victorious battles such as Haastembeck and Closterseven. Led by M. de Grandmaison, the corps captured Harbourg, taking several enemy flags in the process. The uniform shown is based on the 1762 Ms.

GENERALS AND STAFF

F1: Aide-de-camp, 1756-74 The uniform for the usually young officers attached to a general's immediate service was very plain when first introduced – a far cry from that of Napoleon's armies barely half a century later.

F2: Lieutenant-general, 1744-74 The senior generals held this rank and from 1744 wore the blue coat embroidered with gold, with two rows of lace on the cuffs showing their rank. Waistcoats and breeches tended to be red but buff was also seen and velvet breeches were sometimes worn.

F3: Maréchal de camp, 1744-74 The rank of 'camp marshal' is best compared to that of brigadier. It was a junior level general's rank without necessarily direct command over a brigade. One row of lace on the cuffs denoted the rank.

F4: Prince de Conti's Guards, trooper, 1740s The personal guard units attached to princes and senior generals could be quite impressive-looking. According to contemporary descriptions, the Prince de Conti's Guard had his colourful livery, generally styled as the king's Gardes du Corps.

F5: Commissaire Ordonateur, 1760s These administrative officers were assistants to the powerful commissaires des guerres and intendants. They seem to have adopted the grey uniform shown in the 1760s.

F6: Commissaire des guerres, 1746-74 The 'war commissioners' were, in effect, generals of the army's administration, supplies and finances. While serving under senior military generals, they had a certain independence and reported directly to the minister of war in matters of their jurisdiction.

ENGINEERS AND MEDICAL

G1: Engineer officer, 1732-44 Chief engineer the Marquis d'Asfeld selected this distinctive scarlet uniform to identify the engineers and denote that they were a separate entity.

G2: Engineer officer, 1744-55 The engineers attached to the Ministry of War in 1744 were assigned grey uniforms. The black velvet cuffs were introduced at that time.

G3: Engineer officer, 1758-63 After a short interlude wearing the blue and red artillery uniform, the blue coat was kept and black velvet cuffs were restored to the engineers in 1758. In time they would become the traditional colours of engineer corps in many countries.

G4: Apprentice, field hospital, 1757-74 Apprentices were young men attached to surgeons to learn medical practice with the armies. They had the uniform of the medical officers but without lace or embroidery.

G5: Surgeon-Major, La Sarre Regiment, pre 1757 Towns

Garde de Paris, private, 1770, at the drill command 'Posez le fusil à terre' (Ground your musket). This back view gives an excellent view of the archer's bandoleer. (Recueil des chartes…, Paris, 1770)

with major garrisons often had a garrison hospital to care for sick or wounded military personnel.

G6: Surgeon-major, La Sarre Regiment, pre-1757 Regimental surgeons appear to have worn the uniform of their regiment before the regulation of 1757 came into force. Shown here is the uniform of the La Sarre infantry regiment.

CONSTABULARY AND BOURGEOIS MILITIA

H1: Maréchaussée de Lorraine et Barrois, trooper, c.1760 The mounted constabulary in the duchy of Lorraine and Barrois had similar duties to the Maréchaussée de France but wore, until 1766, the yellow livery of the duke, the exiled king of Poland who was Louis XV's father-in-law. Note the pointed ('Polish') cuffs.

H2: Maréchaussée de France, trooper, 1720-56 From 1720 every part of the country came under the jurisdiction of a detachment of this mounted constabulary, the ancestor of the present Gendarmerie in France. There were 30 companies, one for each provincial 'Généralité', but their size varied according to the size and population of the province. Each company was divided and sub-divided into small squads. The dress shown was worn until 1756.

H3: Canonniers de Lille, 1720s These figures are based on a 1729 painting showing the officers and men of this ancient company of artillery in civilian dress but armed with muskets and swords. This reminds us that although many units of bourgeois militia had uniforms, many others did not.

H4: Stratsbourg Bourgeois Militia, 2nd Cavalry Squadron, 1744 The Stratsbourg militia were fond of uniforms, but for the royal visit of 1744 they obviously made a special effort.

H5: Metz Bourgeois Militia, infantry, 1750s The four bourgeois militia battalions of this important garrison city all had this blue and red uniform.

Notes sur les planches en couleurs

A1 Régiment d'Esterhazy, hussard, 1735-43 Ce fut le premier régiment à avoir un uniforme différent du bleu ciel traditionnel. **A2** Régiment de Bercheny, officier, 1735 L'uniforme de ces hussards était plus raffiné et sophistiqué que durant les décennies précédentes. **A3** Régiment de Bercheny, officier, vers 1720. **A4** Régiment de Versailles, hussard, vers 1716 Son uniforme, ainsi que le style des soldats, étaient typique des premiers hussards. **A5** Régiment de Rattsky, hussard, vers 1720 Leur style se rapprochait encore beaucoup des "Hongrois" sauvages.

B1 Régiment de Raugrave, hussard, 1752-1756. **B2** Régiment de Polleresky, hussard, 1744-46 Le premier uniforme de cette unité était couleur cannelle, avec une pelisse verte. **B3** Régiment de Turpin, hussard, 1757-60. **B4** Régiment de Beausobre, hussard, 1752-56. **B5** Régiment de Lynden, hussard, vers 1745

C1 Fusiliers, ou Miquelets des Montagnes, simple soldat Les armes, l'équipement et le costume bien particuliers sont typiques des Pyrénéens. **C2** Arquebusiers du Roussillon, simple soldat Dans un ordre de janvier 1719, l'uniforme était gris-blanc, sauf pour le bataillon de Delio, qui devait porter l'uniforme de la guerre : bleu à doublure rouge. **C3** Fusilier des Montagnes, simple soldat, vers 1740 L'uniforme de cette unité était un mélange d'uniforme conventionnel et de costume régional. Il porte un "berette". **C4** Klendholdt, dragon, 1719-39 Ce soldat de cavalerie porte l'uniforme entièrement rouge qui subsista jusqu'en 1734 environ.

D1 Volontaires Bretons, hussard, 1746-49 **D2** Volontaires de Geschray, fusilier, 1747-59 **D3** Volontaires du Dauphiné, fusilier, 1748-63 **D4** Le Noble, simple soldat et officier des fusiliers, 1735-44 Cette unité était tout d'abord vêtue de gris-blanc, mais adopta rapidement une uniforme bleu. **D5** Dumoulin, dragon, 1738-45 Les dragons avaient tout d'abord un uniforme entièrement rouge, mais vers 1738 des parements verts furent introduits.

E1 Volontaires de Hainaut, simple soldat, 1757-62 **E2** Volontaires de Soubise, chasseur, 1762-63 La compagnie de chasseurs est illustrée dans les Ms de 1762 avec un uniforme vert, mais les dragons et les grenadiers portaient un uniforme bleu. **E3** Volontaires étrangers de Clermont-Prince, soldat des dragons, 1758-63 Leur uniforme était très reconnaissable, avec une capote jaune grège aux parements rouges et un casque en cuivre. **E4** Volontaires de Saint-Victor, hussard, 1761-63. **E5** Volontaires de Flandres, dragon, vers 1762 L'uniforme illustré s'inspire des Ms 1762.

F1 Aide de camp, 1756-74 **F2** Lieutenant-Général, 1744-74. **F3** Maréchal de camp, 1744-74 Il s'agissait d'un grade inférieur de général, avec un rang de galon sur les manchettes. **F4** Gardes du Prince de Conti, vers 1740 **F5** Commissaire Ordonnateur, vers 1760. **F6** Commissaire des guerres, 1746-74

G1 Officier ingénieur, 1732-44 Le Marquis d'Asfeld choisit cet uniforme écarlate très reconnaissable pour identifier les ingénieurs et pour indiquer qu'ils représentaient une entité séparée. **G2** Officier ingénieur, 1758-63 Après un court interlude durant lequel ils portèrent l'uniforme bleu et rouge de l'artillerie, la capote bleue fut conservée et on redonna les manchettes de velours noir aux ingénieurs en 1758. **G4** Apprenti, hôpital de camp, 1757-74 Ils avaient l'uniforme des officiers médicaux mais sans galons ni broderies. **G5** Chirurgien dans un hôpital de garnison, 1757-74 **G6** Chirurgien-major, Régiment de La Sarre, avant 1757 Il semble que les chirurgiens de régiment portaient l'uniforme de leur régiment avant l'introduction du règlement de 1757.

H1 Maréchaussée de Lorraine et Barrois, gendarme monté, vers 1760. La maréchaussée du duché de Lorraine et Barrois porta, jusqu'en 1766, la livrée jaune du duc, le roi de Pologne en exil et des manchettes pointues ("à la polonaise"). **H2** Maréchaussée de France, gendarme monté, 1720-56 L'uniforme illustré fut porté jusqu'en 1756. **H3** Canonniers de Lille, vers 1720 Ces personnages sont des officiers et soldats de cette compagnie d'artillerie très ancienne en uniforme civil, mais armés de mousquets et d'épées. **H4** Milice bourgeoise de Strasbourg, 2e Escadron de cavalerie, 1744 **H5** Milice bourgeoise de Metz, infanterie, vers 1750 Les quatre bataillons de la milice bourgeoise de cette importante ville de garnison portaient tous cet uniforme bleu et rouge.

Farbtafeln

A1 Esterhazy Regiment, Husar, 1735-43. Dies war das erste Regiment mit einer Uniform, die nicht die traditionell himmelblaue Farbe hatte. **A2** Bercheny Regiment, Offizier, 1735. Die Kleidung dieser Husare war ausgefeilter und gepflegter, als das in den vorherigen Jahrzehnten der Fall gewesen war. **A3** Bercheny Regiment, Offizier, 20er Jahre des 18. **A4** Versailles Regiment, Husar, ca. 1716. Die Uniform und die Zusammensetzung des Regiments war typisch für die frühen Husaren. **A5** Rattsky Regiment, Husar, ca. 1720. Der Stil war durchaus noch rauh „ungarisch".

B1 Raugrave Regiment, Husar, ca. 1752-1756. Die Husarenkleidung wurde bis 1756 getragen. **B2** Polleresky Regiment, Husar, ca. 1744-46. Die erste Uniform dieser Einheit war zimtfarben und hatte einen grünen Umhang. **B3** Turpin Regiment, Husar, ca. 1757-60 **B4** Beausobre Regiment, Husar, 1752-56 **B5** Lynden Regiment, Husar, ca. 1745

C1 Fusiliers bzw. Miquelets des Montagnes, Gefreiter. Die recht merkwürdigen Waffen, die Ausrüstung und die Bekleidung war für die Bergsteiger der Pyrenäen typisch. **C2** Arquebusiers du Roussillon, Gefreiter. Laut eines Befehls von Januar 1719 war die Uniform grau-weiß, außer im Delio-Bataillon, welches die Uniform des Krieges tragen sollte, nämlich rot mit blauem Futter. **C3** Fusilier des Montagnes, Gefreiter, 40er Jahres des 18. Jahrhunderts. Die Kleidung dieser Einheit war eine Mischung aus der Standarduniform und der Regionaltracht. Die abgebildete Figur trägt ein „Berrette". **C4** Kleinholdt, Dragoner, ca. 1719-39. Der Soldat trägt die einfarbig rote Uniform, wie sie bis etwa 1734 gängig war.

D1 Volontaires Bretons, Husar, 1746-49 **D2** Volontaires de Geschray, Füsilier, 1747-59 **D3** Volontaires du Dauphiné, Füsilier, 1748-63 **D4** Le Noble, Füsiliergefreiter und Offizier, ca. 1735-44. Die Farbe der zunächst grau-weißen Uniform änderte sich bald zu blau. **D5** Dumoulin, Dragoner, 1738-45. Die Dragoner hatten zunächst eine einfarbig rote Uniform, doch wurden um 1738 grüne Aufschläge hinzugefügt.

E1 Volontaires de Hainaut, Gefreiter, 1757-62 **E2** Volontaires de Soubise, Jäger, 1762-63. Die Jägerkompanie wird um 1762 in einer grünen Uniform gezeigt, obwohl die Dragoner und Grenadiere blau trugen. **E3** Volontaires Étrangers de Clermont-Prince, einfacher Soldat der Dragoner, 1758-63. Die Kleidung dieser Soldaten war unverwechselbar und bestand aus einem gelbbraunen Waffenrock mit roten Aufschlägen und einem Messinghelm. **E4** Volontaires de Saint-Victor, Husar, 1761-63. **E5** Volontaires de Flandres, Dragoner, ca. 1762. Die abgebildete Uniform beruht auf dem 1762er Modell.

F1 Adjutant, 1756-74 **F2** Generalleutnant, 1744-74. **F3** Maréchal de camp, 1744-74. Dabei handelte es sich um einen niedrigeren Generalsrang, der durch eine einreihige Litze an den Manschetten bezeichnet wurde. **F4** Prince de Conti-Garde, einfacher Soldat, 40er Jahre des 18. Jahrhunderts. **F5** Commissaire Ordonateur, 60er Jahre des 18. Jahrhunderts. **F6** Commissaire des guerres, 1746-74

G1 Offizier der Pioniere, 1732-44. Der leitende Pionier, Marquis d'Asfeld, wählte diese unverwechselbare, scharlachrote Uniform, um die Pioniere hervorzuheben und sie als separate Einheit erkenntlich zu machen. **G2** Offizier der Pioniere, 1744-55. Die dem Kriegsministerium 1744 zugeordneten Pioniere erhielten graue Uniformen, die schwarzen Samtmanschetten wurden damals eingeführt. **G3** Offizier der Pioniere, 1758-63. Nach einer kurzen Übergangszeit, in der die Pioniere die blau-rote Uniform der Artillerie trugen, wurde die blaue Jacke beibehalten, und die Pioniere erhielten 1758 die schwarzen Samtmanschetten zurück. **G4** Lehrling, Feldlazarett, 1757-74. Diese Männer trugen die Uniform der Sanitätsoffiziere, jedoch ohne Litzen und Stickerei. **G5** Stabsarzt eines Garnisonsspitals, 1757-74 **G6** Stabsarzt, La Sarre Regiment, vor 1757. Bevor die Vorschrift von 1757 in Kraft trat, trugen die Regimentsärzte offenbar die Uniform ihres Regiments.

H1 Maréchaussée de Lorraine et Barrois, einfacher Soldat, ca. 1760. Die berittene Polizeieinheit im Herzogtum Lothringen und Barrois trug bis 1766 die gelbe Livree des Herzogs, der exilierte König von Polen, mit spitz zulaufenden („polnischen") Manschetten. **H2** Maréchaussée de France, einfacher Soldat, 1720-56. Die abgebildete Kleidung wurde bis 1756 getragen. **H3** Canonniers de Lille, 20er Jahre des 18. Jahrhunderts. Die abgebildeten Figuren zeigen die Offiziere und Mannschaften dieser alten Artilleriekompanie in Zivilkleidung, allerdings mit Musketen und Schwertern bewaffnet. **H4** Strasbourg Bourgeois Militia, 2. Kavallerieschwadron, 1744 **H5** Metz Bourgeois Militia, Infanterie, 50er Jahre des 18. Jahrhunderts. Die vier Bürgerwehrbataillone dieser wichtigen Garnisonsstadt trugen alle diese blau-rote Uniform.